Elements of Train Dispatching

Volume 2

Handling Trains

by

Thomas White

ii

VTD Rail Publishing
3604 220th Place SW
Mountlake Terrace WA 98043
http://www.vtd.net

Printed in the United States of America
by Gorham Printing, Rochester, Washington

ISBN 0-9719915-2-9

Library of Congress control number 2002108973

Thanks to a thorough reading by Stuart Anderson, several small errors
have been corrected in this second printing.

ILLUSTRATIONS

Photographs, drawings, and diagrams by the author except:

Joern Pachl: All cover photos.

Historische Sammlung der Deutschen Bahn AG: 15-1 (bottom)

Cover design by the author.

The cover wrap-around picture and the train dispatcher inset are in the Burlington Northern and Santa Fe Railway (BNSF) control center in Fort Worth, Texas. The cab-view approaching a clear controlled signal is on BNSF west of Edmonds Washington. The combination represents the 2003 version of the pictures on the cover of Volume 1.

The author thanks Burlington Northern and Santa Fe Railway for permission to use the images of its facilities.

The opinions expressed in this book do not necessarily reflect dispatching policies or procedures in use or endorsed by The Burlington Northern and Santa Fe Railway Company.

NOTES ON VOLUME 2

Volume 1 contains an overview of train dispatching and the basic railroad information needed by a train dispatcher. The scope of the information is similar to the knowledge a prospective train dispatcher would have needed to be invited to become an apprentice train dispatcher. Volume 2 contains the information that a prospective train dispatcher would learn while learning to handle traffic, and during the first years of handling trains.

The colon separating hours and minutes (10:00) is not used in train dispatching work. As in Volume 1, time is written as four numbers with no separation (1000). Railroads generally use the twenty-four hour time format (0000 is midnight and the first minute of a day, 1200 is noon, 2359 is one minute before midnight and the last minute of the day). Both conventions are used in "Elements of Train Dispatching". Time between midnight and ten in the morning (1000) has a leading zero to make the time a four digit number (0935).

Train dispatchers encounter two kinds of railroad language; the technical terms and the slang terms. Most of these terms are listed in the Index/Glossary of Volume 1. When new terms are used, they are printed in **BOLD CAPITALS** when initially used and explained. Similarly to Volume 1, the terms are also listed in a glossary that gives a reference to the page on which it was explained, rather than duplicating the explanation.

CONTENTS

11. BACKGROUND KNOWLEDGE

THE TERRITORY

A train dispatcher should be as familiar as possible with the territory being handled. Terrain and track geometry can have a significant effect on the results of decisions made by dispatchers. Knowledge of the terrain can be:

- helpful in determining the running time for a train with a failed unit, station work, heavy tonnage, or other condition affecting train speed and running time,
- valuable in assessing the potential effects of inclement weather,
- helpful with a timely judgment of whether a situation is a problem or an emergency,
- valuable when responding to an emergency.

The more the dispatcher knows, the better the decisions and the reaction to unusual situations will be.

Most railroads once required train dispatchers to make familiarization trips over the territory at least annually. Some, understanding the importance of detailed familiarity with the territory required annual trips and encouraged additional trips, making extra dispatchers available to relieve dispatchers inspecting the territory. Some, making use of the train dispatcher's expertise, also required a report at the end of a familiarization trip, expecting observations, assessments, and recommendations. The advent of system control centers (instead of division dispatching offices) has generally resulted in the reduction or elimination of the requirement of familiarity with the territory and familiarization trips. Frequent familiarization trips are not practical when the territory being handled is hundreds of miles from the dispatching office. There are several ways to see the territory. Each should be used at some time to provide the information that may be possible only from a certain point of view.

- Ride a locomotive. This was once the common method of road familiarization. Listen to the conductor and engineer. They are generally happy to give a train dispatcher a full guided tour.

They will tell of signals that cannot be seen in advance, places that trains cannot be stopped because of road crossings, places where train handling is tricky, places where station work is especially time-consuming and other important information. They may also complain about train dispatchers. If they do, listen to them. Their criticism may be accurate. If it is, consider the criticism and suggestions against your own work. Stand behind the engineer and watch the train handling procedures. Note the combination of tonnage, horsepower, speed, and location. Pay attention to the loadmeter and to airbrake operation with relationship to the terrain. Pay attention to station work. Stay with the engineer sometimes. Drop off with the conductor at other times. Pay attention to how long things take and whether certain stations require an exceptional amount of time.

- Ride a track inspection vehicle. Trains generally move at a much greater speed than a track inspector. The point of view from the locomotive cab is different from the point of view near the ground. The track inspector will also be able to provide a different type of information about the line: areas that are ongoing maintenance problems, areas particularly susceptible to high water, flash floods, drifting snow and other weather-related problems. If the track inspector discovers problems during the trip, ask what the exact nature of the problem is, what the consequence might be, and the magnitude of work required to fix the problem.

- Drive and walk to as much of the line as possible. Drive to every road crossing. Get out and look at the line in both directions. Look at industry tracks, buildings near the track, bridges and any other features. Take notes and pictures. It is often useful to take notes and make sketches directly on track charts and maps. There is nothing specific to look for. There is no way of knowing ahead of time what situation will develop and what information will be required to handle the situation. The driving/walking trips will allow you to see things that might have been missed from a moving locomotive or track inspection vehicle. At some future time while handling an unusual situation, the track chart will stimulate memory of what was seen from the ground, perhaps providing valuable information. If complex trackage extends over a long distance, an effective familiarization trip could involve two train dispatchers and two automobiles. Park one at a convenient place, both dispatchers ride together to another convenient place a reasonable one way walking distance from the first car, park, and walk to the first car.

- Last Resort: Watch a video of the line. The widest-possible-angle lens will not show what a person will see first hand. A video can be a reasonable refresher for a person with good knowledge of the line. It is a poor substitute for seeing the line in person.

Supplement information from field trips or watching a video with maps. Road maps that also show railroad lines can be helpful. The relationship between the railroad and towns or cities and adjacent or intersecting roads can be important in an emergency or when relieving a crew on the road. A named place on the railroad may have no civilization anywhere in sight, and

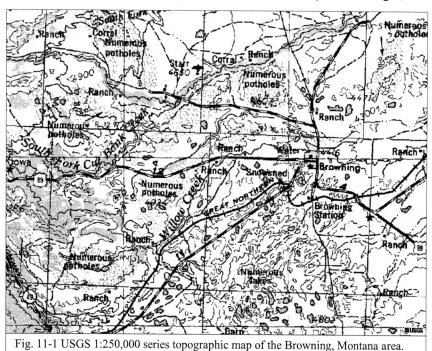

Fig. 11-1 USGS 1:250,000 series topographic map of the Browning, Montana area.

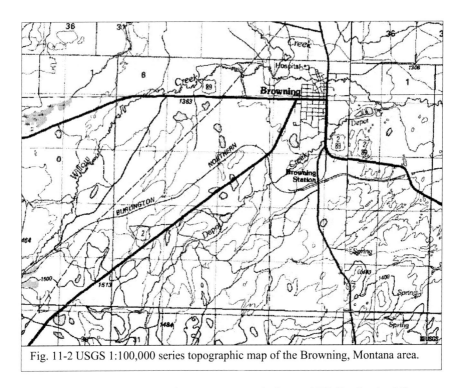

Fig. 11-2 USGS 1:100,000 series topographic map of the Browning, Montana area.

there may be a large town between named places. US Geological Survey topographic maps can also provide useful information. They are available in several different scales and show physical features in detail, including the contour of the terrain. The most detailed of these maps show the location of power transmission lines, unimproved roads and trails, and individual buildings outside of urban areas. The information learned from maps will probably not be useful in daily train operation. In an emergency, it can be valuable.

ACTIVITIES

Predicting the future is an essential element of the train dispatcher's work. The future cannot be accurately predicted without knowledge of the activities involved. Train dispatchers should acquire at least a functional knowledge of the activities that are being supervised, with close attention to the time required to perform various tasks, what is practical and reasonable to

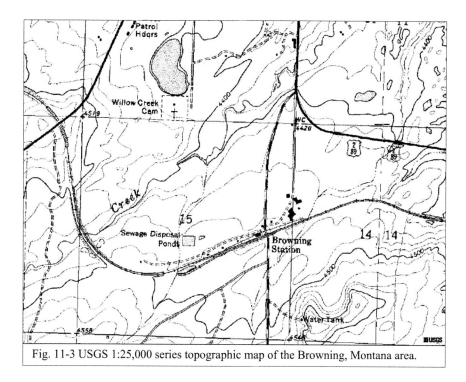

Fig. 11-3 USGS 1:25,000 series topographic map of the Browning, Montana area.

expect, and what is not practical or just cannot be done. Familiarization trip activities should include time with signal maintainers, production track maintenance crews, local track maintenance crews, yardmasters, drawbridge operators and any other people that affect the movement of trains on the dispatcher's territory. Exposure to each of these activities should be part of the training of student dispatchers.

The knowledge of reasonably expected time can be important when allocating time on the track for maintenance work or figuring a train that has station work. Advice from trusted sources is always helpful, however, some caution must be used in generally relying upon someone asking for track authority to provide accurate and objective information. On a busy district, train crews and maintenance workers listening to the situation on the radio may decide that they will never get authority to work unless they can be finished by some specific time or within some specific amount of time. Sometimes they will even convince themselves that the work can be completed in an impossible amount of time. In some cases, a train service or maintenance employee might intentionally ask for a shorter time than necessary to ensure that they can start the work. Once the work is started, generally it must be continued to conclusion regardless of the expiration of the authorized time. In either case, the person providing the bad information is responsible for the bad information, however it is the dispatcher, not the person providing the bad information that must suffer through recovering after the work took longer than expected. Ultimately, a dispatcher may be found partially culpable for delays resulting from granting a request for work that should have appeared unreasonable.

12. PEOPLE

At the fundamental level, train dispatchers supervise people. They
- issue instructions for the movement of trains to train crews,
- issue authority for use of the main track to maintenance of way crews,
- report failure of track and signals to maintenance of way crews.

They also have close working relationships with people who can affect their work;
- exchanging traffic with dispatchers on adjoining districts,
- exchanging traffic with yardmasters, and terminal managers,
- authorizing Maintenance of Way, work train, and local freight train track occupancy for specific periods of time.

Any or all of these people can affect
- how simple or complicated the dispatcher's shift will be,
- how well the dispatcher's plans are executed and thus the quality of the dispatcher's work,
- whether or not the dispatcher makes a mistake that results in admonishment or being out of service for discipline.

Every person among them comes to work, has a job to do, and wants to go home as soon as possible. The ability to do the job and go home is directly affected by the train dispatcher. The ability to come to work can be affected by the train dispatcher in a subtle way.

Consider everyone on your territory to be part of your crew. Each discipline among them has supervisors that have responsibility for and authority over the way in which employees of that discipline perform their work. A higher level of manager such as a Superintendent, a General Manager, or a Vice President may have responsibility and authority for every discipline involved in the operation of the train dispatcher's district. That responsibility and authority is usually indirect, through the managers for each discipline. The train dispatcher directly organizes the employees of every discipline to create transportation, the company's product. That is not a management task of insignificant magnitude. On a given train dispatcher's shift, hundreds of people are performing dozens of essential tasks when and where the train dispatcher directs or allows them to.

Think about yourself on the receiving end of whatever you are doing. You would prefer to not be working for an abusive, authoritarian supervisor that knows nothing of your work. You have integrity and would not do anything to intentionally disrupt the work you are doing or to sabotage a supervisor. You might, however, do exactly what you were instructed to do, even if you knew it was the wrong thing to do. You might not offer a reasonable and productive alternative to an incompetent instruction. You might let your abusive supervisor walk right into serious trouble when a word from you would prevent it. The people who work for you will act the same way.

Learn as much as possible about the work of the employees you supervise. A dispatcher that makes unreasonable demands because of ignorance will not be respected and will probably receive little help from the employees on the district. Unreasonable demands include constantly allowing insufficient time for the work that must be done when more time is available and asking for the physically impossible. Understand that the railroad will probably not employ people for make-work, so the tasks being presented to you by the people assigned to do them are necessary.

Be logical and reasonable in determining when to allow an employee to perform the work. It is unreasonable to call a signal maintainer from home at 0200 for a signal failure, have the person rush to work to fix the problem, then not allow the time on the track to work because there are too many trains.

Be logical and reasonable in assigning work. When train crews know that there is a reason that a train is chosen to make a difficult online move to pick up cars, there will generally be no complaints regardless of the work to be done. When they frequently receive instructions to pick up cars at a location that the train cannot clear and traffic will not allow holding the main track, or pickup cars from a track facing the wrong way with no convenient way to run around, they will complain no matter what the assignment. The answer to a question about assigned work might be "It's a repaired bad order for Denver and you're the only train going that way today" or "You're the first train in two days that won't be in a traffic jam while working there". That kind of answer will be better received than "Because I said so" or "You don't see the big picture, just do it". If the move is unreasonable but you are following instructions, then tell the crew "I have been instructed to tell you to move the ballast empty from the back track at Tyrone to the storage track at Ulster". This may sound petty, but credibility is important. The train crew can have a direct effect on the train dispatcher's workload and performance.

Be decisive at all times without being autocratic. Be tolerant without being submissive. Issue instructions, not requests unless a request is truly appropriate. If you need the train to clear up even though it means cutting a crossing, the instruction is "Take the train in the clear at Zender on arrival", not "you want to clear up when you get to Zender?" or "How about clearing up at Zender?" If the response is "But we'll have to cut the crossing", the answer is "Correct" or "I thought so", not "Well, you want to do that so I can get 6 by without delay?" Never end an instruction with a question mark.

Some employees may respond to an instruction with a threat such as "If you make us pick up that car, we're going to go eat." Some people are like that no matter how well you treat them. Never fight them and don't back down because of the threat. A train dispatcher that does either will be the recipient of an endless array of that kind of response. If the instruction was reasonable in the first place, then let the person carry out whatever it is they are threatening, as long as the threatened action is within the rights of the person threatening. If the crew is entitled to stop the train to eat, let them do it. Build it into the plan. If doing the work and going to eat will cause an hours of service tieup, then if the instruction was reasonable, so is the hours of service tieup.

The employees in the field may have first hand knowledge of a situation that the train dispatcher does not have. If the response to an instruction is a suggestion that doesn't make sense considering the information you have, ask questions. Consider suggestions from employees in the field, but be aware that some may sense weakness and indecisiveness and attempt to talk you into giving their work to someone else or altogether abandoning an attempt to assign some work. If the response is "That car is on the elevator stub behind three and the runaround is full. We're going to need to leave the train out of town, set that car over, respot and use the siding to run around – probably a couple of hours. It would be better to have an East Man get it and take it to Albany yard." The reply might be "They didn't tell me it was over there [or the runaround is full], that's not going to work. Leave it." Or "I know, but it's got to make tonight's 453 from Eugene."

The train dispatcher shouldn't baby-sit or do all of the thinking for the people in the field, although the modern systems generally establish that situation to some degree. A train dispatcher should not take on responsibility that is not required. The favor of informally relieving someone of responsibility could cause a big problem once they are accustomed to it and they find themselves working with another dispatcher who does not know of your favors, or perhaps you are really busy and overlook that little thing you are not required to do.

For example, a track maintenance worker must be prepared to stop the vehicle within the range of vision. The train dispatcher is (generally, depending upon the specific operating rules in effect) responsible for conflicts between trains and track maintenance, but not among track maintenance workers. When the train dispatcher is not responsible for conflicts between track maintenance vehicles, the dispatcher should not attempt to take that responsibility. First, the dispatcher can tell the second maintenance worker on a section of track of the first, but not vice versa. The first and second will not know about the third and so on. If the dispatcher makes a habit of telling the holder of each maintenance authority of all of the others, it will eventually be expected. That situation itself is already dangerous, because not all dispatchers will be providing the favor that is not required. Second, if each maintenance employee is accustomed to being told what to watch for, they will eventually overlook the fact that some inevitably do not know about others and there will be a collision. The same principle applies to instructing a train to proceed at restricted speed. Never append a reason to that instruction. "Proceed at Restricted Speed looking out for train ahead" implies that the dispatcher knows that the reason the signal cannot be cleared is the train ahead. That may be a reason that the signal cannot be cleared, but there may be more than one reason (the signal may be red because of the train ahead and a broken rail and a broken wire and water over the track and a landslide). The train dispatcher cannot know why the signal is red.

Do not take on responsibility is not the same as do not do more than required. Telling a crew that they will be a Nowhere for a while, so they can stop at Town Center for up to thirty minutes before getting in the clear is not required but relieves nobody of responsibility.

Hints are helpful and not dangerous in some situations. For example, in mountainous territory where there are few places to remove a vehicle from the rail, if the dispatcher has a maintenance vehicle that will be traversing the entire section westward, allowing another intending to traverse the section eastward will not benefit the employee wanting to go east. It would not be unreasonable to respond

> *Bill Wilson is out there somewhere coming that way with a Speedswing. You probably won't be able to get by him, will you?*

The maintenance worker may decide to do some other work instead of wasting time waiting for the approaching vehicle. The dispatcher has performed the dispatcher's function of efficient operation without compromising safety. In another situation, a maintenance worker may want authority for a section occupied by one train and about to be occupied by another. Best practice is to tell the maintenance worker to call back after the second train has passed. Some rulebooks may require this procedure rather than issuing authority to follow a train that has not passed. If authorizing in advance track occupancy following a train is allowed, technically, the dispatcher need only authorize the maintenance work following the two trains, after the two trains, or whatever the specific rules require. It is up to the maintenance worker to know that the specified trains have passed. At some time during the conversation, either before or after issuing the authority, a little hint from the dispatcher may keep the maintenance worker out of trouble. After issuing authority following two trains, one of which has definitely passed and one of which hasn't passed or may not have passed, a hint in the form of a question makes sure the maintenance worker will remember the traffic to wait for. The second train may be 10 miles away, but still the dispatcher asks right after issuing the permit "Is that 7943 showing yet?" After the maintenance worker gets back to the truck or gets ready to pull back into the highway to set on or encounters whatever else may be distracting, that question will stick.

This kind of helping hint will find its way back to the dispatcher. After going too strong on a track authority, instead of a repeat, the response from the track maintenance employee may be

> *1130? Mail train fall down some more?*

If the maintenance employee hasn't figured out that the dispatcher may have passed out too much rope, once the dispatcher has figured it out, the call asking for time back will probably result in help if it is at all possible.

If a maintenance worker sounds unsure when asked how much time is needed or the requested time sounds marginal for the task described, ask if more might be needed and offer what is available

> *Next thing up there isn't until 1450. I can give you that much in case it's not working out.*

Or make sure that the maintenance worker understands that the limit being given is real.

> *I can give you the two hours, but 677 will be on the flashing yellow then, so there won't be any more.*

Treat everyone with respect and be careful of familiarity. If it is necessary to address someone by name, use his or her title, or Mr./Ms.

> *Train dispatcher calling Welding Foreman Jones, over.*

or

> *Mr. Jones, I only have until 1320 there. Will that work?*

There is a fine line between informality and familiarity. Informality, such as addressing or referring to people by first name can be effective in managing people if it is appropriate. It the dispatcher knows or has met Welder Foreman Stan Jones, it is not unreasonable to say

> *I'll need you in the clear by 1115 for sure, Stan. 611's got to be in the clear at Detroit for 10 by 1135.*

Or

> *Have you seen Stan Jones? He was going to look at the frog on the east switch and I'm curious if he found anything.*

Familiarity is not appropriate. Whether the person at the other end of the phone or radio is your brother or your neighbor, don't visit and don't make special allowances or grant special favors. Never change an instruction because of your relationship with the person asking, nor give the appearance that you would consider it. If your brother is an inept locomotive engineer that always takes an extra ten minutes heading in, figure it that way. If every train dispatcher on the district knows that your brother will be in the clear within thirty seconds of the figured time every time in any weather, figure it that way.

13. TRAFFIC

The train dispatcher handles two basic types of traffic: trains and maintenance activities. At one time, the dispatcher's involvement with maintenance activity consisted of publishing a lineup. Maintenance forces used the track clearing the times shown on the lineup or protecting against trains. The only other time that the process involved the train dispatcher was when a train was unexpectedly delayed because maintenance forces chose to protect against it, stopping it in the process, so they could continue their work. Train dispatchers now issue specific authority for maintenance of way activity, just as they do for trains. This increases the workload several times, but almost eliminates the surprise of maintenance of way crews stopping trains while protecting the worksite.

FREIGHT TRAINS

Freight traffic is the main or only traffic on most railroads in North America. Freight traffic requires constant attention and is more difficult to handle than passenger trains for several reasons.

- Freight trains do not have a constant size from day to day, and often change during the course of a trip.
- Performance may not be constant from day to day.
- The locomotives assigned to a freight train are generally just powerful enough to move the train over the most difficult grade of the trip. A failure may cause the train to stall. With the locomotives working properly, the speed may vary greatly as the train moves along the line.
- The station work assigned to a freight train may vary from day to day and sometimes during the course of a trip.
- The time that freight trains operate can vary greatly from day to day.
- Once the train crew is on duty, the time elapsed before the train is ready to leave may vary greatly from day to day.

The more the train dispatcher knows about each freight train, the more accurate the plan will be. Accurate planning means less work re-planning and changing things. It also means less work getting out of unintended situations. Often, the details of the train are not offered when the dispatcher is given the call. Even if the train isn't set or the paperwork isn't done, ask for at least an estimate of the train size. "135 cars" or "9600 feet" or "8500 tons" or a combination of those facts is better than no information at all. Any terminal should have this much information before setting a call. Certain intermodal trains may be an exception, but they are generally similar enough every day for initial figuring using a typical train. If the train is a run through from another district, be sure to find out about work at the initial terminal on your district (such as a setout or pickup, engine change or engine servicing) that the outbound crew must do before leaving. Knowing at least an estimate of the train size can tell the dispatcher roughly what running time to expect and where the train will fit. Knowing the train size can also give a basis for estimating when the train will leave the terminal. If the yard tracks are all about 4500 feet and the train will be 8500 feet, the train must couple cars from more than one track, or double, before leaving. That knowledge tells the dispatcher roughly how much time to allow and perhaps whether the train will need to use the main track before leaving or if it will prevent arriving trains from entering the yard.

Sometimes the dispatcher is offered a car count and advice that "he has 10 minutes at Fargo and 15 minutes at Houston". That information may not be sufficient to give an accurate picture of the work to be done. First, the estimate may be unrealistic. Setting out 5 cars on the point into the house track at Fargo may be a 10 minute move. Setting out 5 cars behind 20 on the mill track may require cutting back of crossings, taking the head end to the mill track, setting out, then baldfacing back across the crossings - a 30 minute move. The dispatcher may assume that the cars are for the packing plant at Houston and find out when the train gets to Houston that they are for the stock track. The packing plant switch is on the main, which is clear, but the train with cars to set out and needs the siding, which is occupied by another train, to get to the stock track. Always have the car count of the train leaving each station at which the consist changes. The 30 minutes work may have been picking up 40 empty intermodal flats, adding 1200 tons and 3400 feet to the train. It could also be setting out 12 cars of feed, reducing the train size by 1500 tons and 720 feet. These variations can make a significant difference when planning. Train speed may change if tonnage has changed. The length of temporary speed restrictions will change if the train length has changed. Either can significantly affect running time. If the length changes, the places where the train may be stopped (e.g. between crossings, between interlockings, clear in sidings) may change.

Because train activity varies considerably from day to day, the handling given to each train may also vary from day to day. A given train may be "hot" or not from day to day. Even when a train is "hot" there may not be a crew rested at the next terminal, or the yard may not be able to accommodate the train at the expected arrival time. The dispatcher should always know, as part of keeping terminals and connecting districts informed of expected arrival times, whether a given train can be accommodated at the projected arrival time. Yardmasters and connecting district dispatchers should notify the train dispatcher if an expected train will be delayed on or after arrival. If it is important to know whether a train is actually needed at the projected time, ask.

For example, a track maintenance crew needs 2 hours to weld rail. A hot intermodal train is 1 hour 35 minutes away. Instead of just denying the work request, determine if the 25 minutes is essential to the next terminal or dispatcher district. The terminal may not have a crew rested, the train may be arriving before the pickup is ready, the ramp track may still be occupied by another train or any number of other things that could provide the needed time. Even if the train has a crew and no terminal work, the dispatcher on the next district may be anticipating a 25 minute delay to the hot train due to other circumstances on the territory.

PASSENGER TRAINS

Passenger trains are easier to handle than freight trains because, generally, they have the same consist, the same power, the same work and the same schedule day after day. The running time of passenger trains is generally dependable to the minute.

INTERCITY TRAINS

Among passenger trains, the intercity train is the least dependable. Station stops are generally the variable. Intercity passenger trains can be delayed at stations because the train is too long for the platform and a **DOUBLE SPOT** is necessary, stopping once to load the coach passengers, then again for the sleeping cars. There may be unexpected delays for stocking the diner, watering the cars, loading baggage, or other passenger-related delays. Unlike unanticipated freight train delay in a terminal, which can be an extended time, the unanticipated passenger train delay is generally only a few minutes. When a few minutes is important to determining a meet with an intercity passenger train that is stopped at a station, always ask about anticipated leaving time. Intercity trains, generally having a long schedule, may have a substantial amount of recovery time. If a few minutes delay is important against other traffic, first determine if the train can arrive at the end of the district on time after the anticipated delay. If not, and the train will continue through on another dispatcher's district, ask if the anticipated delay can be recovered.

REGIONAL TRAINS

Regional passenger trains generally do not experience unanticipated station delays. Trains are generally short, thus not needing a second stop at stations, and do not require servicing en route. Regional trains have a short schedule and generally a small amount of recovery time. They are more sensitive to delay than intercity trains, but are easier to plan accurately.

COMMUTER TRAINS

Commuter trains are both easy and difficult to handle. They are easy because they perform exactly the same way day after day. Commuter trains generally operate within a minute or two of schedule throughout the trip. The difficulty is the sensitivity to delay. The schedules are short and there is generally very little recovery time. Commuters, more than any other type of passenger, expect punctual operation.

SCHEDULES

There are two general types of train schedules; operating schedules and transportation schedules. Operating schedules consider every detail of the trip, considering the running time between stations and allowing time specifically for planned meets, passes, and connections. Transportation schedules are much more general in nature, using a desired leaving time at the initial station and generally achievable running times and station dwell times.

OPERATING SCHEDULES

Building an operating schedule can be a labor-intensive and time-consuming process. Difficulty increases as the traffic level increases. Generally, operating schedules can not be constructed individually. Very few trains will not affect the schedule of some other train. Operating schedules must also consider the specific terminal resources necessary to process the train. The operating schedules may be generally identified as three separate plans; schedule, terminal plan, and operating plan but construction of the three segments must be integrated. The completed schedule identifies:

- the source of the traffic for the train, such as industries, connecting trains or intermodal cutoff time. The source of the traffic includes allocation of resources needed to accommodate the arriving traffic such as a receiving track, car inspectors for inbound inspection and the time needed for arrival processing,
- the terminal resources needed to switch the traffic out of the arriving source traffic, including classification tracks, switch engines that process the traffic, and the time needed for the switching,
- the terminal resources needed to consolidate the switched traffic into a train including a track on which to make up the train, a switch engine to make up the train, car inspectors for the outbound inspection and air test, and the time needed for train make up and processing,
- the locomotive for the train including allocation of resources necessary to accommodate the arriving locomotive such as a

service facility track, the personnel needed to inspect and service the locomotive, and the time needed for processing the locomotive,

- the crew for the train including the rest period necessary before reporting for duty,
- track on which to operate between terminals including the time the track is to be occupied,
- track on which to meet, pass, or be passed by other trains including the time the track is to be occupied,
- the terminal resources needed to accommodate the arriving train such as a receiving yard track or the main track for a run-through train and the time the track is to be occupied.

The relative importance of each train is built into the schedule. Trains that are less important are scheduled to clear the way for trains that are more important. An operating timetable generally includes **RECOVERY TIME**. Recovery time is an amount of time (generally six percent to ten percent of the running time) added to running time to mitigate the effect of unpredictable events (e.g. signal failure, temporary track condition, severe weather).

If operating schedules thoroughly consider all of the required elements and if all of the processing time and running time assumptions are correct, the operating schedules form an operating plan that is executable. Operation is only improvised in the case of a failure, using the recovery time in the schedules as needed to restore normal operation. The benefit derived from the effort required to develop operating schedules is that:

- The effort of train dispatchers, yardmasters and others handling elements of the operating plan is generally directed toward executing the plan.
- Attention of train dispatchers, yardmasters, and others handling elements of the operating plan may be generally dedicated to trains that are having a problem.
- The operating plan provides a framework that can be used as the basis of a plan for a train that has had or is having a problem.

- The operating plan will readily demonstrate the effect of a late train on the supply of crews, locomotives, and traffic on other trains.

TRANSPORTATION SCHEDULES

Most train schedules in North America are transportation schedules. Transportation schedules are not as detailed as operating schedules. Their construction requires much less time and effort than do operating schedules. Transportation schedules are constructed from typical running times and typical terminal times. They do not consider interaction with other trains and generally do not consider terminal resources in detail. They may include an amount of time to offset the effects of train interaction. The amount of time may be arbitrary or it may be developed by recording the time typically required for train interaction. Because each train of a transportation schedule is considered individually, schedules may be constructed and changed individually. The completed schedule identifies:

- the leaving time at the initial station,
- the schedule running time between stations,
- the amount of dwell and perhaps the arriving and/or leaving time at stations,
- possibly the arriving time at the final station.

Some transportation schedules, called Elapsed Time Schedules, may specify the time between and at stations without specifying even an initial station leaving time.

Each transportation schedule can generally be executed individually. Because the schedules do not consider interaction with other trains, it may not be possible to operate all of any given two or more trains as scheduled.

The ease of constructing and modifying transportation schedules is offset by

- a significant effort required to constantly improvise and re-plan operation,

- the need to constantly decide which trains will have schedule performance sacrificed for the benefit of other trains,
- the need to determine the effect of new plans on the supply of locomotive, crews, and traffic for other trains.

The relative importance of each train is established by instructions to train dispatchers, yardmasters, and others handling train operations. The handling instructions for a given train may vary from day-to-day or over the course of one trip.

An operating plan based on transportation schedules can result in a situation sometimes known to train dispatchers as *Train du Jour*. A train that has been performing poorly because of decisions made in favor of "hot" trains becomes "hot". The previously "hot" trains become inferior to the *Train du Jour*. The use of transportation schedules can also lead to a situation in which two "hot" trains that must not be delayed by any other traffic encounter each other and there is no correct solution.

PRIORITY

Priority makes a train "hot". Priority can be applied in one of two ways.

Priority may be a tie-breaker. Situation: Opposing trains are both late. Both trains are being given every opportunity to recover time. These trains are given precedence in track allocation unless the other train involved will become late as a result. When they encounter each other, one train will recover the maximum amount of time, the other will not and may become later. Application of priority, or which train is more important in the instant case if all else is equal, will determine which train slows or waits for the other.

Priority may be the deciding factor, as in cases of *Train du Jour*. When priority is the only deciding factor, all other trains slow or wait for the "hot" train as necessary, regardless of consequence. Situation: Being "hot" has put a train five hours ahead of schedule. Another train will cause the "hot" train to lose five minutes of running time if it advanced from Boston to Chicago instead of waiting at Boston for the "hot" train. Waiting for the "hot" train at Boston will be the first of many delays, many of which would not occur if the train is advanced to Chicago. The entire situation may result in a shortage of rested crews or locomotives and ultimately affect operation for many hours. The "hot" train has priority, however, and the other train will wait at Boston.

DELAY

Delay is often the subject of disagreement in the railroad industry. A railroad's definition of delay can affect the general organization and predictability of the operation. It can also affect the way that the dispatcher handles trains. A train may be considered delayed

- when it is slowed from track speed,
- when it is slowed from the maximum speed it can achieve with its combination of locomotive and tonnage,
- when it is stopped,
- when it fails to leave a terminal within the specified time after the crew is on duty.
- when it fails to achieve scheduled running time between stations,
- when it fails to arrive at a station on time or fails to leave on time.

Delay measurement is used to assess the efficiency of operation and the capacity of the infrastructure. Delay is also generally the factor used to determine how trains will interact with each other during planning and execution of the plan.

DATA COLLECTION

Analysis of delay information can help locate operating problems. The application of the definitions should be uniform among the trains being studied to ensure consistent results. Analysis of this information can show the way in which the trains affect each other, and the way in which certain combinations of trains are affected by the infrastructure.

OPERATION

The handling of a combination of trains is generally dictated by instructions that apply priority and a definition of delay. Sometimes, instructions for the priority handling of a train can cause substantial delays without the need to consider the definition of delay. Instructions such as

- never see a [flashing yellow/yellow],
- always [2,3,4,5,6] signals lined ahead of the train,
- no trains ahead within [1 hour, 2 hours, 3 hours],
- no trains ahead within [10 miles, 20 miles, 50 miles, 100 miles]

are absurd, serve no useful purpose, and will cause substantial delays and possibly hours of service tieups. Regardless of the absurdity, instructions from an appropriate authority must be followed. Carefully document the reasons for substantial delays:

> *Boston 1 hour 15 minutes for No. 2 account would give No.*
> *2 a flashing yellow before in the clear at Chicago.*

Generally, however, efficiency of railroad operation is dependent upon which of the definitions of delay is used in planning and in executing the plan. Whether one train or the other has priority is generally subsidiary to the definition of delay when making a train movement decision. The combination of transportation schedules and a broad definition of delay can make the work of a train dispatcher challenging and frustrating as one impossible situation after another is encountered.

Sometimes different definitions of delay apply to different trains. Sometimes a different definition may be applied to a train under different circumstances. Knowing which definition applies is essential when planning traffic.

The delay definition *Failure to arrive or leave on time* provides the greatest flexibility and the greatest general recoverability. If the schedule of an important train has been designed with time for scheduled interaction with other trains and some recovery time, it may be possible to slow or stop the important train for a few minutes to allow a less important train to recover schedule. If a train is due to arrive at 0230 but arrival at 0205 is possible, it isn't delayed unless it arrives after 0230. Defining delay as *failure to arrive or leave on time* can be essential to the overall reliability of operation.

The delay definition *Failure to make schedule running time* can apply to a late train or to a train that has recovery time included in the schedule running time. *Failure to make schedule running time* allows recovery of delayed trains in the same manner as failure to arrive or leave on time. If a train has 2 hours to make a 1 hour 50 minute trip, it hasn't been delayed unless the trip takes more than 2 hours.

The delay definition *failure to make track speed,* applied to a train that is on time or early can allow insufficient power to be a reasonable cause of delay, but can also influence meet, pass, and terminal operation decisions to have significant negative effect on trains. For example, The running time from Boston to Chicago is 40 minutes. A "hot" train that must not be delayed is running from Chicago to Albany. A train moving the other direction lacks one minute of being

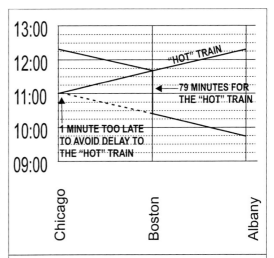

Fig. 13-1 Delay to an inferior train for an opposing "hot" train that cannot be delayed can be up to twice the running time between sidings.

able to run from Boston to Chicago and clear at Chicago without delay to the "hot" train. Since it will delay the "hot" train, it must stay at Boston for 79 minutes instead of moving to Chicago (Fig. 13-1). There may be collateral delays. A second train that might have had time to run from Albany to Boston cannot because of the train at Boston that could not run to Chicago. When a train is late, time must be recovered if possible. *Failure to make track speed* is an appropriate delay definition in this case.

The delay definition *Stopping* is often used but has little value, at least in ensuring the performance of a train. A train may lose running time without being delayed. A non-stop meet may bring both trains from 60 m.p.h. to walking speed, but if they didn't stop, they were not delayed. A train dispatcher may comply with the instructions to not delay (stop) a specific "hot" train and still handle an otherwise impossible situation. If a few minutes makes the difference in advancing an inferior train against a "hot" train and the consequence if delaying the inferior train for an extended time is undesirable, the "hot" train may be slowed at one or two control points in advance of the meeting point by not clearing signals until the "hot" train has reduced speed. The "hot" train is not delayed (stopped) and the railroad is not tied up as a consequence of a lengthy delay to the inferior train. (This is not the preferred nor best way of handling a close meet and is described as an alternative for only when required by the situation.)

It is important for train dispatchers to understand what is meant by "delay" in train handling instructions and how to apply the definition being used to planning and executing the plan. The combination of transportation schedules and a very conservative definition of delay can result in an endless assortment of impossible situations. On a railroad that conducts operations in that manner, the only reasonable course of action for a train dispatcher is to follow the instructions exactly and apply to a supervisor for specific instructions in handling each of the impossible situations.

As with the application of priority handling instructions that leave no choice but substantial delays and perhaps hours of service tieups, document the delays in detail. "No 119 at Kandro 2 hours 30 minutes to let No 5 by" does not tell the same story as "No 119 at Kandro 2 hours 30 minutes to let No 5 by to avoid 5 minute delay to No 5 at Mason and on time arrival at Zeta." Delays are recorded in order to find their way onto reports. The reports are written for people who make train handling decisions (or advise those who do). If those people do not know the consequences of the instructions, the instructions will not change.

HOURS OF SERVICE

Railroad train and engine crews, signal maintainers, train dispatchers, and control operators are subject to the federal Hours of Service law and regulation (49 USC 21101-21108 and 49 CFR 228). Personnel must not be called to duty when they have not had sufficient rest as defined by the law and must not be allowed or required to remain on duty when the legally allowed work period expires. Train dispatchers oversee compliance with this regulation.

TRAIN DISPATCHERS AND OPERATORS

The most immediate requirement is that train dispatchers must not exceed nine hours of duty in any twenty-four hour time period (If there is only one shift, meaning only one person working the office in a day, the limit is twelve hours). Under normal circumstances, the implication is that after an eight hour shift, the dispatcher must be off duty for 16 hours, or two shifts. If the dispatcher is relieved of duty for one hour or more (known as a **RE-LEASE**), the clock stops while the dispatcher is off duty. When dispatchers must work more than eight hours because of late relief or to make up for a shortage of personnel, the 9 hour requirement requires some careful consideration.

One extra hour on duty at the end of a shift does not present a problem as long as the next day's shift begins at the regular time. One extra hour of duty at the end of a shift and one extra hour of duty prior to the beginning of the next shift is ten hours within a twenty-four hour period and is a violation. An extra hour at the end of a shift after a one-hour release is acceptable, but the next shift cannot be followed immediately by an extra hour. Caution must be used when deviating from regular shifts to ensure that nine hours is not exceeded in *any* twenty-four hour period; any point in time to a time twenty-four hours later.

Hours of service requirements are the same for operators as they are for dispatchers. The hours of service regulations do not apply to Assistant Chief Dispatchers, Chief Dispatchers, Managers of Train Operations and similar positions as long as they do not directly handle train movements. Work under more than one section of the hours of service regulation (train/engine service, train dispatcher/operator, signal maintainer) or in service covered by and not covered by the regulation (**COMINGLED SERVICE**) is covered entirely by the regulation. All railroad service during that tour of duty is covered regardless of the order in which the covered and non-covered service occurred. All three sections of the regulation apply simultaneously; none is superseded by another.

Should someone on one of the supervisory positions relieve the dispatcher and handle trains for any period of time, the hours of service regulations apply to the entire tour of duty of that person. If a person works in train/engine service and as a train dispatcher during the same tour of duty, all of the work performed during that tour of duty applies to calculation under both sections of the regulation.

Examples:

The Chief Dispatcher goes on duty at 0700. The regular first trick dispatchers work 0800 until 1600. At 1500 one of the first trick dispatchers must leave because of a family emergency. The Chief Dispatcher may handle the position until relieved by second trick at 1600, but must be off duty at 1600, nine hours after coming on duty. If the Chief Dispatcher began work at 0600, relieving the trick dispatcher at 1500 would be a violation. Similarly, the Chief Dispatcher begins work at 0600 and one of the first trick dispatchers is late arriving because of a traffic accident on the way to work.

A train dispatcher holds dual seniority as a locomotive engineer. After working a full shift as a train dispatcher, the train dispatcher is asked to start the shift of the yard engine because the engineer is late for work. Under the part of the regulation that applies to locomotive engineers, eight hours of the allowed twelve have been worked. Under the part of the regulation that applies to train dispatchers, eight of the allowed nine have been worked. During this workday, the train dispatcher may work no more than one more hour under the train dispatcher section of the regulation and no more than four more hours under the locomotive engineer section of the regulation. Both apply simultaneously, so the train dispatcher may work only one hour as a locomotive engineer.

Train dispatchers and operators are required to maintain the records of their hours of service and generally must monitor their own compliance.

TRAIN AND ENGINE CREWS

The hours of service regulation for train and engine service is more complex than the regulation for train dispatchers and operators.

They must not be on duty for more than twelve hours in any twenty-four hour period.

A release, during which the clock stops, is four or more hours at a designated terminal (generally meaning the "home" or "away from home" terminal for the crew district).

There is an exception to the designated terminal requirement. When employees are prevented from reaching a designated terminal by

- a casualty,
- a track obstruction,
- an act of God,
- a derailment or major equipment failure resulting from a cause that was unknown and unforeseeable to the railroad carrier or its officer or agent in charge of that employee when the employee left the designated terminal,

a release of four or more hours may occur at a place with suitable facilities for food and lodging.

The clock resets after 8 continuous hours off duty except if the employee was on duty for twelve hours, the rest period must be ten hours instead of eight hours.

Time spent in transportation from the place of reporting to the point of assuming duty is counted as time worked.

An outside local is tied up at Outskirts. The conductor becomes ill and must lay off. The source of supply for the district is City. It is a two hour drive from city to Outskirts. An extra board conductor is called for 0700 to arrive at Outskirts in time for the 0900 on duty time of the local. A van service is used for transportation. The conductor rides as a passenger. The time between 0700 and 0900 is on duty time for the conductor. The conductor's hours of service limit is 1900. The engineer came on duty at Outskirts at 0900 and has until 2100.

Time spent in transportation from a duty assignment to the point of final release is neither time on duty nor time off duty. The time waiting for transportation to the point of final release after a duty assignment is also neither time on duty nor time off duty.

The extra board conductor on the Outskirts local will return to City at the end of the shift. The two hour trip from Outskirts to City is not time on duty, so the conductor may work at Outskirts until 1900. The trip back to City is also not time off duty, so the required rest period does not begin until the conductor ties up at City at 2100.

It is important to note that time on duty and time off duty for the purpose of compensation may not be the same as the time on duty and the time off duty for the Hours of Service regulation.

A crew on duty at 0800 runs out of time at 2000 but has not reached the terminal at which the crew will be released from duty. Transportation arrives at the train at 2115. The crew arrives at the terminal and is released from duty at 2230. For the purpose of the hours of service regulation, the crew was on duty at 0800 for twelve hours and rest began at 2230. They may be on duty continuously from 0800 until 2230, depending upon the specific labor agreement in effect, for the purpose of pay calculation. In another example, again depending upon the specific labor agreement in effect, a crew has been on duty for five hours on arrival at the terminal. They have sufficient time to work back on a train in the opposite direction. A train is due at the terminal five hours later. If the crew remained on duty, they would not have sufficient time to work back to the initial terminal. If they have eight hours off duty, the train will be delayed for three hours. They are released for five hours then work back to the initial terminal. They are off duty at the original terminal after ten hours on duty and require only eight hours rest, however, labor agreements may provide that the crew is paid continuously including through the five hour release because they have not had a complete eight hour period off duty.

Generally, if the time off duty is eight hours or more, the time off duty is not compensated and the return trip is a separate day's pay.

When a crew's hours expire on the road, prompt relief is essential. Failure to relieve the crew promptly may
- completely tie up the railroad if the train is not in the clear when the crew's hours expire,
- cause congestion if the train is left in a siding needed for meeting and passing trains,
- cause a shortage of crews for other trains,
- be a violation of labor agreements.

Train dispatchers directly affect the time that train and engine crews are on duty, their transportation to the point of final release and the waiting time until transportation arrives. They often establish the time that train crews are called on duty, they affect how long the crews take to get over the road, they arrange for relief of crews that cannot reach the terminal in the allowed twelve hours, and they notify terminals of arriving traffic. Except when a computerized information system keeps the required records, train dispatchers maintain the records of the hours of service of train and engine service employees. Computerized systems may provide confusing or misleading information about hours of service for other than a simple workday consisting of a continuous tour of duty handling a train. Regardless of misleading information to the contrary, the crew will stop when their time expires. This may have the same effect on traffic movement as a derailment. If the hours of service information is provided by an automated system, be sure to understand the way in which it calculates the information it presents. If there is any doubt, ask the train or engine crew specifically "What time do your hours of service expire?"

Failure to pay close attention to the hours of service can cause serious problems for the dispatcher and for the railroad. Attempting to avoid a crew relief by attempting to bring a train to a terminal with minutes to spare may result in a complete tieup of the line or at least a tieup of the terminal.

SIGNAL MAINTAINERS

The hours of service regulation for signal maintainers is generally less complex than for train and engine service employees. Signal maintainers must not go on duty or remain on duty:

- Unless the employee has had at least eight consecutive hours off duty during the prior twenty-four hours;
- After the employee has been on duty for twelve consecutive hours until the employee has had at least ten consecutive hours off duty;
- After the employee has been on duty a total of twelve hours during a twenty-four hour period or after the end of a twenty-four hour period whichever comes first, until the employee has had eight consecutive hours off duty.

As it is in the application to train and engine service employees, the definition of on duty and off duty is complex:

Time on duty begins when the employee reports for duty and ends when the employee is finally released from duty.

Time spent performing any other service for the railroad carrier during a twenty-four hour period in which the employee is engaged in installing, repairing, or maintaining signal systems is time on duty. The previously described principle of comingled service applies.

A train dispatcher has dual seniority as a signal maintainer. At the beginning of a shift, the dispatcher is rested and has nine hours of duty available. At the end of an eight hour shift, the dispatcher is needed to perform service as a signal maintainer. The train dispatcher regulation allows nine hours of duty in twenty-four, so one hour remains. The signal maintainer regulation allows twelve hours of duty in twenty-four. Both are in effect simultaneously. The dispatcher may work one hour as a signal maintainer, which complies with both regulations.

A clerk in the signal department is qualified as a signal maintainer. A shift of clerical work begins at 0700 after eight hours off duty. At 1100, the clerk must perform work as a signal maintainer for two hours. At 1300, the clerk returns to clerical duties. There is no limit to hours of clerical duties. A signal maintainer is limited to twelve hours in a twenty-four hour period. Regardless of whether the service after 1300 is clerical or signal maintenance, no more than six hours of service remain until there has been a period of eight hours off duty.

Time spent returning from a trouble call, whether traveling directly from the work location to the employee's residence or from the work location to the employee's residence by way of the employee's headquarters is neither time on duty nor time off duty. There is one exception. Up to one hour of the time spent returning from the final trouble call occurring during a period of broken or continuous service is time off duty.

A signal maintainer lives thirty minutes from a case of trouble. The trouble is cleared at 0300. If the signal maintainer returns to duty before 1030, it is the same twenty-four hour period; the time off duty began at 0330. If no period of duty has begun before 1100, the period of duty that ended at 0300 was the final trouble call of a period of broken or continuous service and the travel time between 0300 and 0330 is time off duty.

In the above example, the signal maintainer lives three hours from the trouble location. If the signal maintainer returns to duty before 1100, it is the same twenty-four hour period; the time off duty began at 0400. If no period of duty has begun before 1100, the period of duty that ended at 0300 was the final trouble call of a period of broken or continuous service and the travel time between 0300 and 0400 is time off duty.

If at the end of scheduled duty hours, an employee has not completed the trip from the final outlying worksite of the duty period to the employee's headquarters or directly to the employee's residence, the time necessarily spent in completing the trip to the residence or headquarters is neither time on duty nor time off duty.

> The signal maintainer's headquarters is at A. The assigned shift is 0700 until 1500. The signal maintainer finishes testing at F at 1430 and returns to A. The signal maintainer is delayed by traffic and arrives at A at 1530. On duty time ends at 1500; off duty time begins at 1530.

If an employee is released from duty at an outlying worksite before the end of the employee's scheduled duty hours to comply with the hours of service limitation, the time necessary for the trip from the worksite to the employee's headquarters or directly to the employee's residence is neither time on duty nor time off duty.

> The signal maintainer's headquarters is at A. The assigned shift is 0700 until 1500. The signal maintainer works on a case of trouble at B from 0100 until 1300 and must then be off duty. Time off duty begins on arrival at A.

For each of the previous three cases, transportation in an on-track vehicle is time on duty. If the signal maintainer returns to A by rail instead of by road, the signal maintainer must arrive at A before the allowed hours of service have expired.

A regularly scheduled meal period of at least thirty minutes but not more than one hour is time off duty and does not break the continuity of service. A release of more than one hour is time off duty and breaks the continuity of service.

> The signal maintainer shift is 0700 to 1530 with a meal period of 1130 to 1200 (thirty minutes). A case of trouble requires the signal maintainer to continue working beyond the end of the shift. The period of duty is considered continuous, the limit of time on duty is 1930, and the off duty period must be at least ten hours if the signal maintainer works until 1930.

The signal maintainer shift is 0700 to 1600 with a meal period of 1130 to 1230 (sixty minutes). A case of trouble requires the signal maintainer to continue working beyond the end of the shift. The period of duty is considered continuous, the limit of time on duty is 2000, and the off duty period must be ten hours if the signal maintainer works until 2000.

The signal maintainer shift is 0700 to 1600 with a meal period of 1130 to 1231 (sixty-one minutes). A case of trouble requires the signal maintainer to continue working beyond the end of the shift. The period of duty is not considered continuous, the limit of time on duty is 2001, and the off duty period must be eight hours if the signal maintainer works until 2001.

An employee may work an additional amount of time not more than four hours on duty when an emergency exists and the work of the employee is directly related to the emergency. The emergency ends when the signal system is restored to service.

Train dispatchers can directly affect a signal maintainer's hours of service. If a signal maintainer is working at a location accessible only by on-track vehicle, the train dispatcher must allow the signal maintainer to return from the work location and clear the track prior to the expiration of the signal maintainer's hours. When a train dispatcher calls for a signal maintainer outside of the signal maintainer's normal shift because of a failure, the signal maintainer's available hours pass even if the dispatcher has not allowed the signal maintainer to reach the failure, has not allowed the maintainer to work at the failure site, or has not allowed the signal maintainer to return from the failure site. Railroads seldom employ extra signal maintainers as they do extra train and engine crews. If the signal maintainer's hours of service expire, there may be no signal maintainer available to repair other failures, or a signal maintainer may need to be brought from another territory, extending the time that the signal system is causing problems for train movements.

Signal maintainers are responsible for their own compliance with the regulation and must maintain the required records; however, they must notify the train dispatcher of the amount of time they have left to work when in a position that could result in the train dispatcher causing a violation.

EMERGENCIES

The regulation provides exceptions for emergencies. The governing law (49USC 21102) excludes situations involving any of the following:
- a casualty,
- an unavoidable accident,
- an act of God,
- a delay resulting from a cause unknown and unforeseeable to a railroad carrier or agent in charge of the employee when the employee left a terminal.

It is very important for train dispatchers to understand that FRA applies a very narrow scope to emergencies. Failure to plan and failure to act promptly do not fall within the scope, and the extent of the emergency is limited to the first opportunity to change the situation.

In the southwestern US, a flash flood may occur at a location distant from the local condition that caused it. Regional conditions that can cause flash flooding can be predicted, but the location and nature of the flooding generally cannot. If the track is impassible due to flash flooding of this nature, the situation is an emergency for the application of the hours of service limitation.

In the southeastern US, flooding often accompanies extended rainstorms. Rivers rise at a moderate rate and the flooding is predicted by the weather service. If the track is impassible due to predicted flooding, or local flooding that is a result of an extended period of heavy rain, the situation is not an emergency for the application of the hours of service limitation.

If a train encounters a situation listed in the exclusions from compliance between stations and the time on duty reaches twelve hours at that location because of the occurrence, it would be permissible to require the crew to remain on duty long enough to take the train to the first point at which it could be left clear of the main track provided that no relief crew could reach the point at which the train stopped before the line was cleared. Had there been time for a relief crew to have been ordered and transported to the stopped train before the expiration of the allowed time of the original crew, instructing the original crew to clear the main track would probably be considered a violation.

If a train is delayed by an incident described in the exceptions, continues beyond the first point at which it could clear the main track, then subsequently reaches the hours of service limitation between stations, requiring the crew to continue to a place at which the train can be left clear of the main track would be considered a violation.

As with the provisions for emergencies in the law as it applies to train and engine service, an emergency as applied to signal maintenance is narrowly defined and does not include any situation that could be anticipated or prevented. For example, track surfacing or tie replacement frequently damage track wires. After the maintenance work is complete, a period of time is required for repair of the signal damage. The time spent repairing the damage is not an emergency and does not qualify for the four hour extension of the hours of service limitation.

MAINTENANCE

Arranging track maintenance is a very important function of the train dispatcher. The world of railroad track was once a simple place. The rails consisted of 39 foot sections (designed to fit in a standard 40 foot long gondola car) bolted together by four or six bolts and two specially forged angle bars. The local section gang of a half dozen men could perform virtually any track maintenance without affecting train traffic. Dispatchers were not concerned with maintenance activities. They issued lineups that the maintenance forces used as authority. If no train was due, they could work. If a train was due, they had to be clear or protect against the train. They traveled on small self propelled vehicles that could be easily removed from the track in a very short time at any of the many setoffs along the line designed for the purpose. If they could not be clear, one of the crew would walk down the track in the direction from which the train was approaching and use torpedoes, fusees, lights, and flags to stop the approaching train. The dispatcher was unaffected by track maintenance, as long as the lineup was accurate, unless the foreman of a crew elected to stop a train. Usually there were repercussions sufficient to make such a surprise unusual.

Train dispatchers must generally pay as much attention to track maintenance forces as they do to trains because they are generally directly responsible for track maintenance. Welded rail, concrete ties, concrete road crossings and other substantial construction methods make track maintenance a time-consuming task. Maintenance once performed by a local gang, such as tie replacement or raising a low spot is often performed by a large "production gang". Heavy cars damage switch points and frogs, requiring frequent welding, which sometimes takes many hours of work.

Handling track maintenance is a delicate balance. The requested time may delay trains, but denying the requested time may result in a speed restriction that will also delay trains. Denying the maintenance request may also result in the condition being aggravated and the track being taken out of service until repaired.

INSPECTION

Track must be inspected for defects on a regular basis. The frequency of inspection is dependent upon the class of track, defined in the Track Safety Standards (49 CFR 213). Generally, mainline track is inspected on a daily or alternate day basis. The track inspector generally drives a hyrail vehicle and travels the length of the assigned territory. Often, the inspector will travel the entire assigned territory in one direction, lay over for the night, then return the next day. The movement of a track inspector is often as predictable as a train and should be planned as such.

UNDER TRAFFIC

Some track maintenance is performed "under traffic". The work generally does not continue as trains pass, but the track can be cleared quickly on the approach of a train. The foreman in charge of the work crew makes a request, generally the previous day, for protection in the form of a written instruction, such as a track bulletin:

MEN AND EQUIPMENT ON MAIN TRACK
BETWEEN MP 308 AND MP 308.5
STOP AT RED FLAG AND DO NOT PROCEED UNTIL AUTHORIZED
BY FOREMAN IN CHARGE.

Dispatchers should pay close attention to work under traffic. The work is safe because no train may pass through the limits without permission of the foreman. Train movement is unpredictable for the same reason. The foreman may let a train continue at track speed, give the train a speed restriction, or delay the train. Dispatchers should keep the foreman in charge of work under traffic informed of train movement in the same manner as terminals and dispatchers on connecting districts. Inquire about the anticipated effect to trains and plan accordingly.

OUT OF SERVICE

Most track and signal maintenance will require that the track be out of service for some amount of time. The work will require authority to use the main track and trains will not be able to run until the authority is relinquished. Track out of service maintenance is the most difficult and labor intensive traffic a dispatcher handles. The difficulty comes in the surprise generally associated with the request. Day shift dispatchers are often inundated with requests for time to work on the track, one after another. Often, the request will be for important work that must be done, but will cause a significant change to the plan. There may not be time for re-figuring before the next request.

It is important to stay ahead as much as possible. Whenever possible, get the day's itinerary from track maintenance forces when they come to work in the morning. They often do not recognize the need for advance information and planning.

Several small maintenance projects are needed on the foreman's territory. The work scheduled for today is a three hour project in the siding at Buffalo and a two hour project between Chicago and Detroit. Similar work needs to be done in the siding at Chicago and the siding at Detroit, but the foreman is not planning on that work for today.

The foreman calls the dispatcher at 0800 asking for three hours in the siding at Buffalo. There will be a freight train in at Buffalo from 1015 for a meet. The dispatcher asks if 2 hours 15 minutes will work. The foreman responds that it will take at least 3 hours. The dispatcher tells the foreman to call back after the train leaves the siding. The train leaves at 1040. The foreman calls the dispatcher for authority on the siding and begins work. The work is finished at 1345. If the crew drives to the work location between Chicago and Detroit, they will arrive at 1430 with not enough time left in the workday for the work that must be done. The crew performs three hours of maintenance work in their eight hour workday.

At 0800 the main track was available for the time required for that work, including the travel time. The sidings at Chicago and Detroit were also available. The foreman did not tell the dispatcher about other work. The dispatcher did not ask. The maintenance crew could have spent at least five hours on maintenance work and perhaps six or seven hours.

Train dispatchers can maximize maintenance productivity by asking about all of the work that a foreman can do on the territory. Maintenance foremen should be encouraged to call for a work plan for the day as early as possible. The dispatcher should consider the work the foreman has to do, the work the foreman would like to do, agree on a workplan for the day and include the maintenance work in the operating plan.

TRACK CONDITONS

Train dispatchers have no direct control over track conditions. They do have direct control over the effect of track conditions. Dispatchers should be aware of the locations of speed restrictions caused by a track condition. If a maintenance foreman requests time for work at or near the location of a speed restriction and there is any question of the ability to authorize the requested time, an important consideration should be whether the work eliminates the restriction.

> A foreman asks for 3 hours between Buffalo and Chicago. An important train is just under three hours away. The foreman says he may be able to clear in time for the important train but is not sure. The request may ordinarily be denied, but the dispatcher asks if the work will remove the 10 m.p.h. speed restriction between Buffalo and Chicago. The foreman responds that it will. The speed restriction has been delaying trains for 15 minutes. If the work is finished and the restriction is removed, the foreman's work can delay the important train for 15 minutes, effectively with no delay. The slow track condition will not affect subsequent trains. Granting the time even with the possibility of a delay to an important train is beneficial under these conditions.

Dispatchers will often need to call maintenance forces to repair a track condition. Often, the indication of trouble is a signal failure. The signal maintainer may not arrive at the failure location for an extended time. Generally, signal failures delay traffic but do not prohibit traffic. The signal failure may cause traffic congestion, however, as trains continue to approach the location of the failure at normal speed, catching trains that are moving slowly through the failure. Regardless of the congestion and possible delay, the signal maintainer should be given authority to work as promptly as possible on arrival.

- Signal maintainers are subject to hours of service regulations. Consuming those hours by requiring the signal maintainer to wait for traffic may cause the signal maintainer to reach the hours limitation before the trouble is found or corrected.
- The signal trouble may be caused by a track condition that could be dangerous but has not been detected by the crews of trains moving at restricted speed. If the condition is not dangerous, it may be become dangerous as trains continue to pass over it.

- The signal maintainer was specifically called to the location for maintenance work. The work is not a surprise. The signal maintainer's time should be used as productively as possible.

If the signal maintainer reports a defective track condition is causing the signal trouble, the dispatcher should call for the track maintenance forces immediately. Trains should not be operated over the defect until it has been repaired. If a qualified maintenance employee (49 CFR 213.7 specifies the qualifications of an employee who may authorize movement over defective track) arrives before the rest of the work crew and authorizes train movement with a speed restriction, the dispatcher may move trains through the area. For reasons similar to those for allowing the signal maintainer to work promptly on arrival, the dispatcher should be careful to avoid delay to the work crew when they arrive.

To the extent possible, the dispatcher should plan on the expected consequences of a failure. Bunching trains should be avoided. Trains moving away from the problem should not wait for trains moving toward the problem. Bunching trains because of the problem should be avoided to the extent possible. To the extent possible, estimate the time that the track will be out of service for the repair and incorporate that time into the plan.

When a crew has been called to repair a broken rail or other condition that requires extensive work with the track out of service, authorizing a time much longer than possibly needed will help keep the crew productive and perhaps reduce the amount of time that the track is out of service. Requiring a crew to call for more time may delay the work. The failure causes enough work for the dispatcher in traffic problems. Adding to that work by requiring a crew to call for a time extension adds unnecessarily to the work. When a foreman reports for authority to repair a condition that makes the track impassible during repair, authorize much more time than may be necessary for the work given perfect conditions. Conditions may not be perfect. For an hour's work, issue 4 hours or more and instruct the foreman to report clear promptly on completion. Also, ask the foreman for a good figure on completion whenever it becomes predictable. It is better to use a short figure that is accurate than a longer figure that is not. For example, on arrival at the broken rail the foreman says that the track should be available in an hour because the task at hand generally takes an hour. Thereafter, problems occur (the right size rail is not available, the rail saw is not working) and the one hour task turns out to be four hours, but all of the movement plans are based on the track returning to service in one hour. A preferable arrangement is a call from the foreman when the time for the remaining steps is predictable with some certainty:

> *We have the rail cut and in place, have the joint bars and we're bolting the joints and spiking now. We'll have the railroad back to you in about thirty minutes.*

The train dispatcher should understand the conditions associated with the foreman's initial estimate of the time the repair will be complete. The foreman's initial assessment of the situation may include time for anticipated problems, such as the need to travel some distance to obtain the correct rail, bars, or tools. This information is also valuable. Use the initial figure for planning, and ask the foreman to advise when everything is at hand and completion is predictable with greater accuracy.

14. FIGURING TIME

Joe gets on a train in New York at 3:30 pm that travels at 62 m.p.h. for 12 hours and stops at Toledo and Gary for 33 minutes each. Bill gets on a train in Los Angeles at 8:40 am that averages 48 m.p.h. for three hours and 67 m.p.h. for 7 hours. What time will it be when Bill and Joe meet in Shreveport, LA?

Remember that kind of problem from math classes in school? The good news is that this is not how you figure time.

PREDICTING THE FUTURE

"Predictions are hard, especially about the future."

Niels Bohr

A significant part of the dispatcher's work is predicting the future. Meeting and passing points are set by predicting ahead of time where the trains will encounter each other. Track maintenance time is allocated by predicting when trains will pass the maintenance location. Crews are called on duty at terminals, locomotives are assigned, and deadhead crews or equipment are ordered based on a prediction of when the train will arrive or be ready.

RUNNING TIME

Learning the running times is part of learning a territory. A new dispatcher on a territory, whether experienced or novice to the profession, will be given a table of running times and other notes, known as a crutch, by an experienced dispatcher on the territory. The crutch shows the running time between each important place (station, siding, interlocking, etc.) on the territory. If running times differ among the types of trains on the territory, the crutch will show the running time for two or more general types of train.

Experience will show how to adjust the typical running times for individual trains. The running time may be affected by the tonnage of the train, the length of the train, the engineer of a train, the type of locomotive or even the specific locomotive on the train, fog, rain, wind, temperature.

Often a rule of thumb can be made for the first estimate of a train that is not similar to one of those for which there is a known running time. A few examples:

- One Horsepower Per Ton (HPT) on level track 50 m.p.h,
- One-half HPT on level track 35 m.p.h,
- One HPT per each percent of grade 15 m.p.h.

The district may have locations that can be used as an indicator of the expected running time elsewhere. The best example of this type of area is a section of several miles of constant grade on a territory that has one or more similar sections, but with different grade. The speed and running time for the train will have the same relationship as the grade. If the grade where the speed has been measured is greater than the grade where the speed is unknown, the speed on the unknown grade will be higher:

The speed is 20 m.p.h. on a 1.2 percent grade, on a 0.8 percent grade, it will be:

*20 m.p.h. * (1.2 percent / 0.8 percent) = 30 m.p.h.*

Running time will be less by the same proportion:

The time between 2 points on a 1.2 percent grade is 30 minutes, on a 0.8 percent grade it will be:

*30 minutes * (0.8 percent / 1.2 percent) = 20 minutes.*

The running time may be affected by a slow order. There are two parts to estimating the running time effect of a slow order; the effect of the slow order speed limit and the effect of reducing to the slow order speed limit and returning to normal speed. The additional running time for the first part is easily calculated:

The distance is the length of the restriction plus the length of the train. For a 30 mph restriction 0.1 miles long and a train 5000 feet long where normal speed is 60 mph:

Train length in miles = 5000/5280 = 0.95 miles.

Restriction length in miles = 0.1 miles restriction length + 0.95 miles train length = 1.05 miles

At 30 m.p.h., the time will be

Hours of travel = 1.05 miles / 30 miles per hour = 0.035.

*Minutes of travel = 60 minutes per hour * 0.035 hours = 2.1 minutes.*

If the normal speed for the train is 60 m.p.h. through the speed limit zone, the normal running time is:

Hours of travel =1.05 miles / 60 miles per hour =.018

*Minutes of travel = 60 miles per hour *.018 hours = 1.1 minutes.*

Additional running time is the difference:

2.1 minutes Time at slow order speed – 1.1 minutes time at normal speed = 1.0 minutes.

Estimating the effect of braking to the slow order speed limit and returning to normal speed is not quite as straightforward. The running time effect of acceleration and braking is related to the rate of acceleration and braking of the train. Unlike other relationships that have been described in this chapter, the rate of acceleration and braking is specific to the train and location. The rate of acceleration is related to the ratio of horsepower per ton (HPT) and the grade. The braking rate is related to the weight of the train and the grade. Since a long train may be moving on different gradients (even uphill and downhill) simultaneously, the rate of acceleration or braking may change as the train moves.

On a constant grade, the difference among trains can be significant. As grade changes, the difference in rates of acceleration or braking for an individual train can be significant. The following table contains some examples of (approximate) rates of acceleration.

Horsepower Per Ton	Level	0.9 Percent Ascending	0.9 Percent Descending
0.9	8 mph per minute	5 mph per minute	10 mph per minute
2.6	15 mph per minute	11 mph per minute	17 mph per minute
3.4	17 mph per minute	13 mph per minute	20 mph per minute

The following table contains some examples of (approximate) braking rates.

Tons	Level	0.9 Percent Ascending	0.9 Percent Descending
3,500	64 mph per minute	69 mph per minute	53 mph per minute
7,800	32 mph per minute	38 mph per minute	21 mph per minute
13,000	26 mph per minute	33 mph per minute	16 mph per minute

Calculating the rate of acceleration and braking for a train requires sophisticated calculation that requires more time and resources than a train dispatcher has available. There is a relatively simple way to estimate the running time effect of acceleration and braking, however.

Determine a location that has topography similar to that of the location in question, a speed limit change, and the ability to measure running time. For example, The speed limit is 40 mph for the eight miles between Albany and Buffalo except for a one mile long curve with a thirty mph speed limit. The 5,000 foot train being considered in this example can maintain track speed on this section of the line, so it will be reducing from 40 mph to 30 mph and returning to 40 mph.

Were there no loss of running time for braking and acceleration, the running time between Albany and Buffalo would be figured:

Amount of 40 mph operation = 8 miles-(1 mile 30 mph + 0.95 miles train length) = 6.05 miles

Hours of travel at 40 mph = 6.05 miles / 40 mph = 0.15 hours

Minutes of travel at 40 mph = 60 minutes per hour * 0.15 hours = 9 minutes

Amount of 30 mph operation = 1 mile 30 mph + 0.95 miles train length = 1.95 miles

Hours of travel at 30 mph = 1.95 miles / 30 mph =0 .065 hours

Minutes of travel at 30 mph = 60 minutes per hour *0 .065 hours = 3.9 minutes

Running time Albany to Buffalo without braking or acceleration time = 12.9 minutes

The actual Albany to Boston running time for this train (or a similar train) is 16 minutes. Reducing speed by ten mph and returning to the original speed increased the running time by three minutes. The slow order in the partially completed example on page 45 is a reduction of 30 mph from 60 mph to 30 mph.

Additional braking and acceleration running time for 10 mph speed reduction = 3 minutes

Additional braking and acceleration running time for 30 mph speed reduction = (30 mph / 10 mph) = 3 * 3 minutes = 9 minutes

The total amount of additional running time for the 30 mph slow order (page 45) is

Additional time at slow order speed = 1 minute

Additional time reducing to slow order speed and returning to normal speed = 9 minutes

Total additional running time for slow order = 10 minutes

This method of calculation is not scientifically correct or accurate, but is sufficiently accurate for the purpose and an answer can be obtained quickly.

Experience can eventually replace much, but probably not all, of the calculation.

TIME STOPPED

The time the train is stopped to be met or passed or for station work must be added to the running time. Additional time for braking and acceleration must be added as described above.

WHEN WILL THE TRAIN ARRIVE?

The answer to that question is important each time that a conflict between two trains must be resolved, each time authority is issued for maintenance work, each time a crew is to be called for duty, and each time someone asks for a figure to use in planning their work. The question will probably need an answer dozens of times for each train the dispatcher handles. The accuracy of the answer each time it is developed will affect some other aspect of operation on the dispatcher's district.

WHEN MUST THE TRAIN ARRIVE?

When determining a meeting or passing point for two trains or determining how much time to give to maintenance of way work, delay must often be considered because sometimes delay cannot be avoided. Sidings or cross-overs do not naturally occur at the points where trains would encounter each other if left alone. Track maintenance cannot always be conducted in the time available between trains. When determining which train to delay when figuring a meeting or passing point or determining whether to allow track maintenance forces or trains to wait, there are four important considerations.

Schedule

If it is a scheduled train, can it arrive at the next schedule point or at the end of your district on time if it is delayed the anticipated amount? Schedule performance is important. Important trains generally have schedules that are less tolerant of delay than unimportant trains, however schedules often have recovery time, extra time intended to allow for events that could not be planned when the schedule was written.

If it cannot arrive at the next schedule point or at the end of your district on time, can it leave on time? Sometimes more terminal time is allowed in the schedule than is required.

If it cannot leave the next schedule point or the end of your district on time, can the dispatcher on the next district arrange for the recovery of the time? The next district may have light traffic, no opposing traffic more important, extra time in the schedule, or extra time in the schedules of opposing trains.

Hours of Service

If the train is delayed the anticipated amount, will the crew have time to get in and tie up before the hours of service limit? If they do not have time and the reason for the possible delay is important enough to justify the cost of a relief crew, is a relief crew available? If a relief crew is not available, is there a place to leave the train with no crew that will not interfere with other train movements and otherwise cause problems?

Call Figure

The call figure is also called a final because it is the dispatcher's final prediction of when the train will arrive. The connecting crew and crews for connecting trains are called on duty using that figure. Dispatchers on adjoining districts will figure meets, passes, and track maintenance work using that figure. The call figure should have considered every foreseeable event. The train should arrive on or within a few minutes of the call figure. If something changed after the call was figured, give arrival on the call figure very strong consideration. If the new situation makes delay to a train that has been called in necessary, notify the terminal (and the dispatcher on the adjoining district if the train is continuing through) of the delay as soon as possible. If alternatives are being evaluated including making a train late on call, discuss the situation with the terminal and/or the other side and determine the effect of a delay.

Delay

The definition of delay that is applied to train handling instructions may supersede the other three considerations. If important trains are considered delayed when they do not make the shortest possible running time and train handling instructions prohibit delay, then delay is the only consideration.

EXPERIENCE - THE PREDICTION TOOL

Merely being present for a train dispatching shift, issuing movement instructions and filling out paperwork does not constitute experience. Every time the future doesn't happen as predicted, there is experience to be gained. Three very important elements are required:

- Know what is happening. You will never sharpen your prediction skills by passing out blocks of time. Learn the detail of everything you authorize. When a train crew reports that they have 20 minutes work at a station, find out what the work is. Learn exactly what is taking 20 minutes so that on the day something has changed, you can adjust your prediction. When a maintenance worker asks for an hour between here and there, find out what the work is and where the work is. Understand the conditions that can make the same work take more time or less. Learn to predict what work will be necessary when possible. The track inspector moves along the line just like a train. Understanding that the employee asking for an hour here and two hours there and another hour somewhere else is actually moving along the road at a generally constant speed toward a specific goal will be of great use in planning.

Understanding the work to be done can increase the productivity of track maintenance forces. A signal maintainer may need two hours for a 30 minute job because the only way to reach the work location is on the track and there is no way to remove the truck from the track at that spot. The signal maintainer may spend the day calling back for the unavailable two hours, or the dispatcher may suggest breaking the two hours into running to some other location where the track can be cleared, making a second run to the work location to do the work and return to the intermediate spot then finally return to the original location. The dispatcher may also suggest that the signal maintainer drive to another location beyond the work location from which a train may be followed immediately, allowing more productive time on the track than may be had by waiting for the train to arrive, then running in the opposite direction to the work location.

- Notice that the future didn't happen as predicted. *If a train is not at a place where you expect it at the time you expect it – look for it.* This advice appears twice in these pages. It is important. Noticing that a train is 30 minutes late on the call figure only when you get the OS from the terminal is as useful as not noticing at all. The crew that was on the train when it lost 30 minutes of your figure is gone. The delay report may not provide a clue. Often, the delay report kept by a conductor doesn't have the kind of detail needed to explain why the train took 30 minutes more than you predicted. Did an engine fail? Did your miscalculation of another train at a meeting point cause the lost time? Did the last pickup take longer than expected? If you didn't notice when the time was lost, you will probably never know, and will have gained no experience. The same advice applies to maintenance work on the track. If track authority expires at 1400 and is not reported clear by 1405, try to find out why. If the authority is cleared 20 minutes late and you merely acknowledge, perhaps with a severe voice, you may never learn about the condition that the employee noticed and stopped to investigate, or the fact that the employee has difficulty estimating the time required.

- Find out why it didn't happen as predicted. This could be as simple as asking when you notice that a train is not where you think it should be or track maintenance is not finished when expected. It could also take remembering the circumstance over a period of time. One engineer may be proficient at train handling and can arrange to slow a train for a restriction so that the restriction speed is reached just as the engine passes the speed sign. Another engineer may not handle a train with the same precision, slowing well in advance. One conductor may be very proficient at car handling, arranging all of the moves required for local work at a station like a choreographer arranges the movements of dancers. Another conductor may make unnecessary engine movements or perform the tasks at a station in an order that is less efficient. One track maintenance worker may spend less time than another at the same task for the same reason: a difference in skill level. The clue that you should be watching from day to day is the answer "No, everything's fine, dispatcher" when you notice that the running time or the station work or the track maintenance is taking too long. Knowing how long work takes gives a basis for the level of confidence placed in a request for time. Some employees don't have a clue how long the work will take and will invent an amount of time because one is required. Others may ask for 30 minutes, knowing that 30 minutes is available and more is not, then proceed with work that takes an hour. When train movement instructions involved time rather than absolute authority, these situations were less of a problem. Predictable events such as trains running from terminal to terminal with no work on the way were published as a schedule. Everyone else was required to be clear of the track at those times. When authority is absolute, the time limit is effectively a guide with little meaning. When time runs out, the work continues until finished.

15. PLANNING AND MOVING TRAFFIC

"Intellectuals solve problems, geniuses prevent them."

Albert Einstein

ELEMENTS OF A PLAN

The plan should consider all of the requirements and reasons for running a train. It should accommodate all predictable events. The realm of the unpredictable should be limited to events such as equipment failure, accidents, derailments, and sudden extreme weather changes.

SCHEDULE

The movement of a train is defined, described, and measured by location and time. Schedule defines the movement of a train by assigning time to events (arrive and leave) at locations. Schedule is used to describe a train (due to arrive at Albany at 1130) and to measure the performance of a train (thirty minutes late arriving at Albany). The train dispatcher allocates time to trains (the amount of time between arriving at Albany and leaving will be thirty minutes instead of zero) and takes time from trains (the time between Albany and Galveston will be fifty minutes instead of one hour ten minutes), modifying the schedule (or defining the schedule of an unscheduled train). The goal of the planning process is generally to have the greatest number of trains possible operating on time. Trains that are late should be late by the least possible amount.

Train schedules are often constructed without a great degree of precision. Sometimes an individual schedule cannot be achieved. The running time may be too short or an insufficient amount of time may be allowed for work at stations. Sometimes one or more of a combination of trains cannot remain on time if all begin on time because the schedules were constructed with no consideration of other traffic that would be encountered.

Train dispatchers should be aware of these situations and consider their effect when planning. When schedules present an impossible situation, the train dispatcher should apply to the chief dispatcher or equivalent supervisor for an acceptable resolution.

DELAY

The definition of delay that is used in evaluating train operation will affect the planning process significantly. If a train that leaves and/or arrives on time at schedule points is not considered to have been delayed regardless of slowing or stopping between schedule points, planning and executing the plan is relatively straightforward. If trains are considered delayed when they do not make minimum possible running time regardless of schedule and train movement instructions prohibit delay to certain trains, planning and executing the plan can become very difficult. Instead of being one of the components of a plan, delay becomes the only component of a plan. The other elements of planning become obstacles that constantly interfere with the plan because they were not considered when the schedule was designed.

PRIORITY

Priority is a very important concept in traffic planning and in handling trains. Priority is most effective when designed into the timetable, not when it is the determining factor in operation regardless of the schedules. Depending upon how priority is used on a given railroad, it may be a tool or the single defining element of planning and operation. Among the elements of planning, the implementation of delay and priority have the greatest effect. When priority is the greatest consideration and delay has the most strict definition, the result can easily be congestion that causes extreme delay to all but a few important trains. The congestion caused by basing all decisions on priority can result in unavoidable delays to high priority trains.

OTHER PLANS

The planning of terminal supervisors and of dispatchers on adjoining territories may affect the handling of one or more trains. If a train is due to arrive at Albany at 1000 and the yard cannot accommodate it until 1045, arriving on time at the expense of making other trains late, making other trains later, or not recovering time on late trains makes no sense. Sometimes *responsibility for the delay* causes the wrong decision to be made. When a train will be held out of a yard due to congestion, it is counterproductive to advance it to the yard entrance at the expense of other traffic in order to be certain that the delay can be shown as "arrived on time, held out of yard". The train being held out of the yard will be blocking other traffic, further degrading service. In addition to documenting delays, the train dispatcher should carefully document reasons for decisions (e.g. *Detroit 30 min meet grain empty account Albany cannot handle until 0930 due to MofW in yard*).

As soon as possible after receiving new planning information from a terminal or adjoining dispatcher district, the train dispatcher should examine each train time for compatibility with the current plan. The terminal or adjoining dispatcher should be notified immediately if there is time to return on any train. (Returning time is notifying the person previously responsible for the train's movement that it may be delivered to you at a later time without affecting its movement on your territory.)

The time that can be returned may be the result of a conflict at the entrance to the terminal or endpoint of the adjoining dispatcher district. For example, the terminal lineup shows train 921 ready to leave Albany at 1000. Train 921 cannot leave until train 2 arrives at 1035. The terminal at Albany or the adjoining dispatcher may be able to use the time to help work in the yard, to help track maintenance, or to help another train. The terminal or the adjoining dispatcher may arrange traffic so that train 921 is ready to leave on train 2's arrival at 1035 instead of waiting thirty-five minutes after it is ready to leave.

It is also possible, however, that the new lineup figure from the terminal is an indication of a situation contrary to the train dispatcher's plan. Train 2 may have no place to go when it arrives at 1035 unless train 921 has left. For example, if train 2 is going through on connection, there may not be a track for train 2 if train 921 is still on the main track at Albany. The siding or one of the main tracks may be out of service. If train 2 has work at Albany, train 921 may be occupying the track that train 2 must use. Train dispatchers should investigate such situations as soon as they become apparent, develop a plan to handle the conflict, and notify all appropriate personnel (e.g. connecting district dispatchers, yard and terminal managers, chief dispatcher).

The time that can be returned may also be found at some other point. For example, train 921 may be able to leave Albany at 1000, but at Detroit, 30 minutes away, a track maintenance crew will not finish repairing the switch until 1120. Train 921 will wait at Detroit for 50 minutes. The train dispatcher should offer the 50 minutes, or as much as is certain to occur, to the terminal or adjoining district dispatcher.

MEET

Almost every meet on a single track line will result in a loss of running time for one or both of the trains. Typically, train dispatchers consider a "good meet" to be one in which the total train delay was minimized. They consider the best situation to be one in which both trains arrive at the meeting point simultaneously. In many cases, this assessment of a "good meet" may be accurate, however it is not always the suitable assessment. If a "good meet" causes a scheduled train to become late, it was probably not a good meet.

Unless the turnout does not require a reduction in speed and the siding is long enough to eliminate the need to slow or stop at the far end, the train taking siding will lose running time even if it doesn't stop. Time is lost braking to turnout speed, approaching the signal at the far end of the siding prepared to stop, and accelerating to track speed. A non-stop meet may delay a train for ten to fifteen minutes depending upon the speed limit. If the train holding the main track passes the first siding switch before the opposing train is clear at the other end, it will lose time slowing for the approach signal and preparing to stop at the far end of the siding. A non-stop meet may also mean a delay of ten to fifteen minutes for the train on the main.

The same principle applies to a meet on two or more tracks. When trains are moving opposite directions on the same track and one will cross over to another track, the turnout speed limit may affect the train crossing over. If the train crossing over is not clear of the crossover before the opposing train reaches the approach signal to the crossover, the opposing train will lose time slowing for the stop at the crossover.

The effect of a meet may vary from one siding to another on a dispatching district. A train moving on a steep ascending grade may be moving at a speed not affected by heading into a siding for a non-stop meet. A siding on or adjacent to a curve that restricts train speed will not have the same effect as a siding on a part of the line with no speed restrictions.

When one train must clear for another without slowing the other train, the ideal meeting point will be where the train taking the siding clears just before the other train must begin slowing.

The time consumed in meeting must be considered when evaluating every meet. A train can leave on time and arrive at the distant terminal late, never stopping for a meet. Train dispatchers must be aware of the relative location of each of the two trains and how one affects the other at the meeting point.

PASS

Calculating the point at which one train will overtake another is similar to calculating a meeting point. The dispatcher must consider what each train is doing as it approaches the passing point. Ideally, the slower train will not head in for the faster train until a point at which it can clear just before the following train must begin to slow because of overtaking it. On a multiple track line, the ideal point at which to cross over to another track to allow a following train to pass is evaluated the same way.

YARD OPERATION

In terminal areas and at some intermediate stations, yard operation must make extensive use of the main tracks, often conflicting with train operation. When the railroad is operated by priority (rather than schedule), yard movements on the main track have the least priority and the greatest delay. Those same local freight and yard operations may be assembling today's "hot" trains or delivering cars that arrived on yesterday's "hot" trains. They may be clearing track room for a "hot" train yet to arrive or yet to be built. They have an operating cost that is deducted from revenue just like that of any other train movement. They should be made as productive as possible. The same principle applies to local freight trains. Local freight trains provide the function of yard engines at stations where no yard engine is assigned.

Yard movements often come as a surprise to the train dispatcher. The crew or the yardmaster announces that the yard engine is ready to do something now. Often, it can't be accommodated now because traffic on the main tracks is already committed to a plan that prevents the yard engine movement. This arrangement sometimes results in a train being unable to enter the yard until a yard engine that must use the track the train is waiting on leaves.

Whenever possible, the train dispatcher and the yardmaster or other person in charge of yard movements should work together to plan main track operation of yard engines. No movement should ever be a surprise just as no arriving train should be a surprise to the yardmaster.

At the beginning of a shift, train dispatchers handling yard and terminal areas should ask the yardmaster or other person in charge of yard operation about expected movements needing the main tracks. The yardmaster will know what work involving the main tracks must be done, but probably not exactly when. The yardmaster's schedule at that time will involve "first thing", "after coffee", "after lunch", or "before they tie up". That's close enough for initial planning. If the general time does not look good, the dispatcher may suggest to the yardmaster

> *The mail is going to be down there about 1330 with the passenger right on his block. That probably won't work until 1350 or so.*

Sometimes the yard movement is not flexible. The train dispatcher should plan traffic to accommodate the inflexible yard movement to the extent possible. In conferring with the yardmaster at the beginning of the shift, the yardmaster may say

> *The 0730 job needs to be at the auto yard at 1430 to drag 452's autos back here.*

That yard engine movement is as "hot" as train 452. The dispatcher should plan that movement in the same manner as train 452 will be planned later in the day.

A yard movement at a specific time may be important to yard operation. A joint train dispatcher/yardmaster planning effort may result in the yardmaster providing a running track in the yard for a through train, allowing a yard movement on the main track without either waiting for the other.

TRACK MAINTENANCE

Track maintenance forces and train dispatchers often have a strained relationship. Track maintenance forces always want to take the track out of service for work (or so it seems). Train dispatchers always say no because there are trains to run (likewise). Both are right and both are wrong. Without trains, there is no need to maintain the track. Without track maintenance, the trains would slow for more and more defective track and eventually be unable to run. Track maintenance and train operation must be integrated if the railroad is to continue operating.

Some track maintenance is planned well in advance. It may not be thoroughly-planned or well-planned, but it is planned nonetheless. This type of planning is generally applied to crews known as "production gangs". They have dozens of workers and a large number of sophisticated track maintenance machines. Planning generally consists of

> *System tie gang 32 will have a window to work on the River Subdivision between Houston and Joliet 0700 to 1700*

Monday through Thursday from June 18 through June 30.
They will close up each day as directed to let No. 8 and No.
65 pass.

The train dispatcher's role is simple, at least between 0700 and 1700. Give the foreman authority and a figure on No. 8 and No. 65. The dispatcher's role is generally simple only in theory. The actual situation at 0700 may include trains that are still in the limits and "hot" trains that were delayed during the night and must not be delayed for the gang. Often, other traffic will be "rescheduled", which is easy to do with transportation schedules. At 1700 there will be many trains to run, but planning their movement is not generally part of maintenance planning. The train dispatcher must develop a plan for handling the accumulated traffic.

Train dispatchers have no control over this "planned" trackwork. They can control "unplanned" trackwork to a greater degree. Every day there are frogs and points to weld, ditches and culverts to clean, signal equipment to check, track to inspect, and other ordinary maintenance duties. Train dispatchers seldom know about these activities until the foreman calls for authority. Just as surprise yard operation is precluded by already committed train movement, surprise track maintenance is often precluded by already committed train movement.

Generally, there are several necessary maintenance activities awaiting each crew. The maintenance supervisors select work to do each day using criteria important to them. Often, whether the track will be available is not one of the criteria. To the extent possible, train dispatchers should plan activities with maintenance forces at the beginning of the shift. Find out not only what they plan to do and when, but what work needs to be done. With thorough planning, it is possible that a crew will stay productive all day on work that must be done, although not necessarily the intended work. Find out about essential projects. If a frog must be welded today or require a speed restriction, arrange the time to weld the frog. Plan the work with the foreman. His plan may be some small projects along the line working their way to the location where the frog needs work. Driving directly to that location and working their way back instead may fit into the traffic plan better than the intended agenda.

Track inspectors move like trains. They start at one end of their territory and move on the track to the other end of their territory in a very predictable fashion. To the extent possible, the track inspector should be included in the plan in the same manner as a train.

EQUIPMENT

Trains and the equipment needed to run a train are interdependent. There is a limited supply of locomotives, cars, and rear end devices for all of the trains that are operated. Trains that do not have the required equipment will not run regardless of schedule. Trains arriving at a terminal with equipment needed to operate trains that are leaving are as important as the trains they carry equipment for. During the process of obtaining information, the train dispatcher should find out if trains on the road or expected to operate are bringing the locomotives or rear end devices required for trains that are expected to leave a terminal. If the dispatcher plans around a train leaving Houston at 1230, the yard based the 1230 figure on a locomotive from train 630 at 0900, and the dispatcher's plan has changed bringing train 630 into Houston at 1100, the 1230 figure on the train leaving Houston is no good. Train dispatchers should ensure that they understand the relationship between the trains they are handling and the expected trains shown on the lineup. That may involve directly asking yardmasters, chief dispatchers, and other supervisors whether lineup figures are dependent on equipment brought in by trains the dispatcher is handling.

CREW

Trains and the crews needed to run them are also interdependent. The supply of crews is often more limited than the supply of equipment. The connection between trains and crews is closer and the balance is often more delicate. Depending on the length of the crew district and the nature of the terminal, a crew may require 4 or 8 hours off duty before handling a train in the opposite direction. They may also need additional time for transportation between the lodging and on-duty locations. If a crew ties up on hours of service, it will not be available for 10 hours or more. In some cases, a crew arriving on a train may remain on duty and handle a train in the opposite direction on continuous time. When a crew will be used on continuous time it is essential that the crew arrive in time for the returning train unless delay of that train is inconsequential. The crew must have sufficient time left under the Hours of Service regulation to return to the home terminal.

Each train arriving at a terminal represents the crew for a train to be run in the opposite direction at some time in the future. The train dispatcher should understand the relationship between the arriving trains and the crews for trains scheduled to leave the terminal. If the crew plan and the traffic plan are not consistent, they must be made to be consistent. That could mean changing the handling of individual trains or changing the crew plan. The chief dispatcher or other individual planning crew utilization may elect to deadhead a crew or change the order of trains leaving a terminal in lieu of expediting or delaying the movement of a specific train.

The availability of a crew for hours of service relief can affect train handling decisions when a train's ability to make the terminal within the hours of service limit becomes marginal. If there are no relief crews, a train may be handled more expeditiously if its ability to reach the final terminal is marginal. If a train is marginal, there is an ample supply of crews, and there is unassigned station work along the line that may require an extra train (or expected traffic will make the work impractical at the time it is usually done), the cost of assigning the work to the marginal train and relieving may be less than the cost of running another train later.

The train dispatcher should be aware of the relationship between the crews of trains being handled and projected trains. If a train will become marginal for an hours of service tieup, decisions should include the crew supply. If a train cannot make the terminal or is marginal, running the train as far as the crew can go may be a poor choice. For example, if a train cannot make the terminal, it is better to tie up on a siding that is ten minutes from the next siding (leaving available sidings twenty minutes apart) in either direction than proceeding closer to the next terminal and stopping on a siding from which the next siding is twenty minutes in either direction (leaving available sidings forty minutes apart). If the train cannot make the terminal or is marginal and the crew is needed for another train, consider the difference between rail and highway travel time. Stopping the train a greater distance from the terminal, but at a location that allows faster arrival of the crew at the terminal may be better than moving the train as far as the crew can make it but with a later arrival at the terminal.

A dispatcher regularly assigned to a position may become familiar with the characteristics of individual crewmembers. One conductor may always have a problem with local work and spend twice as long as anyone else for the same work. One engineer may be able to get every second of running time out of a train without speeding while another loses time being cautious because of inability to judge stopping distances. Dispatchers should also include these characteristics into planning.

THE TERRITORY BEYOND

Dispatchers should include adjoining dispatchers' territories and adjoining terminals in the plan for the district, not just use the published times in formulating their own plan. If you can't move a train at the time that shows in a figure published to you, tell the adjoining dispatcher or terminal when you can move it. The adjoining dispatcher may be delaying 4 eastward trains and/or stopping track maintenance in the process of getting the westward train to you on that 1530 figure. A simple one-sentence remark to the adjoining dispatcher or terminal that published the figure can make a big difference:

> I can't use that 1530 grain drag until 1620.

may enable the dispatcher on the other side to use the time for opposing trains or for maintenance of way work.

WHEN TO FIGURE A PLAN

Figure a plan as soon as a prediction doesn't match the event *If a train is not at a place where you expect it at the time you expect it – look for it.* First, find out why the prediction didn't match the event. The reason could be important to developing a new plan (e.g. engine failure, signal failure, train has fifty cars more than the consist shows) Once you know the location and projected activity of the train, compare the new information to the plan. If the new location and projected activity will not work within the current plan, build a new plan. The new plan may not involve more than a few changes in meeting points. It may involve a complete change in strategy, with changes in meeting points, crew call times, crew assignments, station work, track maintenance and other activities.

Train dispatchers in North America are typically not provided with any type of planning software. The planning must be done on paper. Depending upon the amount of traffic and the complexity of the situation, an experienced train dispatcher may do a significant amount of planning entirely mentally. Learning to plan on paper is important on all but the simplest territories. A train dispatcher handling simple territory should know how to plan on paper if there is a possibility of working a busier territory in the future.

There are two commonly used planning methods; trainsheet and diagram.

TRAINSHEET

The trainsheet has been the standard planning tool of train dispatchers in North America for over 100 years. The principle is simple. Plan in pencil, writing figures as if they were OSes. For each train on the territory and each train expected, write a figure wherever an OS is expected. On territory where OSes are not provided and are not regularly recorded from CTC indications, pencil figures on the sheet at stations an hour or less apart. The end of the planning period (the planning horizon) should be no sooner than the latest time that a train currently on the territory will complete its trip. As the planning process goes on, projected stops for traffic may result in a longer trip than expected for some trains. The last train to complete its trip may do so later than the expected end of the planning period, resulting in an extension of the planning period.

Mark the expected times and locations of yard moves and track maintenance. These notes can be made in the station column in the center of the sheet, in the appropriate station row.

Fig. 15-1 The "old way"; Chicago Illinois 1969 (above) and Dresden East Germany 1980 (below). The same profession, similar tools, but one plans and records with a trainsheet, the other with a diagram.

After recording where/when each train is expected to be, record

Fig. 15-2 The "new way"; Magdeburg Germany 2002. The dispatcher has a modelboard display, the bottom row of screens, similar to North American train dispatchers. The top row of screens are the "electronic trainsheet"; diagrams that display a record of train movements as well as a projection of train movements that can be manipulated for planning. Unlike the pair of photos in Fig. 15-1, there is no equivalent picture for the "new way" of planning in North America.

where/when each train is scheduled to be. Write the schedule time as a figure at each schedule point. If a train has an elapsed time schedule, write on time figures calculated from the initial leaving time.

DIAGRAM

The diagram is the standard rail traffic planning tool virtually everywhere in the world except North America. A diagram is a time/distance graph. One axis is the distance, with station locations marked. The other axis is time. A diagram may have horizontal (stations on the x-axis) or vertical (stations on the y-axis) orientation. For many years, a diagram was used to plan operating schedules in North America. The grid of time and distance was permanently mounted on a board. Pins were stuck into the board at the appropriate time/distance points for the schedule times of trains. The pins were connected by string stretched along the pins for each train, hence the name stringline diagram.

The preparation method for a diagram is the same as it is for a trainsheet. Only the mechanics of the format are different. Mark the figured path of each train through time and distance on the diagram. Mark the difference between figure and schedule by marking the schedule time points for each train. Mark all of the expected yard operation and track maintenance on the diagram.

YOUR OWN PIECE OF PAPER

The trainsheet was, in addition to the dispatcher's planning tool, a required record of train operation. That part of the trainsheet's function is widely understood and recognized. The planning function is not. Some railroads have replaced the trainsheet with "electronic trainsheet" systems. These systems provide a place to enter all of the required record information. They allow display of the information. They typically do not show the relationship between trains and do not allow planning figures to be used. On a railroad using an "electronic trainsheet" system, a dispatcher should consider drawing a simple trainsheet or diagram on a paper and photocopying it for use as a planning tool.

HOW TO FIGURE A PLAN

Two planning methods are discussed; "scheduled railroad" and "strict priority"; both using transportation schedules. "Strict priority" operation involves the most restrictive definition of delay (a priority train has been delayed if it does not make the minimum possible running time) and a prohibition of delay to any train for a train of less priority. Schedule is ignored in "strict priority" operation (except that early operation of high priority trains is considered good). The discussion will involve an example of each of three types of operation:
- single track ("scheduled railroad" only),
- double track, current of traffic, sidings,
- double track, bi-directional signaling, no sidings.

For each of the three examples, Albany and Galveston are large terminals that can accommodate all trains on arrival without affecting other trains except as specifically stated.

The discussion is an introduction to the process, so it will be limited to basic elements of planning. The examples do not consider turnout and siding speed limits, time lost due to acceleration or braking, the location of street crossings that must be kept clear, the handling characteristics of individual trains of the same type, the effect of weather on running time and on the time needed for station work, and other conditions or events that affect train operation. Planning with a trainsheet and with a diagram are both demonstrated. The trainsheet and diagram examples show the appearance of the sheet or diagram at the end of the associated discussion. Dark lines and figures represent records of movements (written in ink). Light lines and figures represent projections (written in pencil).

The examples begin "from scratch" building a plan without reference to any previous planning. To the extent possible, figures that have been published should be a timetable to be followed when planning. The best planning and published information are of little value to anyone using the information if the entire process is started from scratch every few hours, causing the "new" lineup to bear no resemblance to the "old" lineup.

Planning is an iterative process. A change in a train, such as a stop for a meet or track maintenance, may affect other trains. Some trains may be affected directly. Others may have a secondary effect because of a change in a train that was directly affected. Each of the affected trains must be re-figured.

Start with the train closest to its final station on the district. Examine the opposite side of the sheet for any trains it will encounter on the same track. Examine the same side of the sheet for any trains that will overtake it. Examine the center of the sheet for trackwork and yard operation. Look for conflicts with the track maintenance and yard operation that have been noted. Continue the same process with each train in the order of its proximity to the end of the trip on the district. Note each conflict on the sheet.

If the district has two or more tracks, there should be no trains in the opposite direction that have a direct effect. That could change when track maintenance, yard operation, and overtaking have been figured. If there are trains in the opposite direction that must be considered, start with the first train to be encountered. Find the meeting point. If the meet slows or stops either train, change the pencil figures for the train for the remainder of the trip.

Once the conflicts are identified, go over the trains in the same order penciling in the times necessary to eliminate the conflicts. Continue the process until all conflicts have been resolved.

PLANNING EXAMPLES

Following are five planning examples representing a single track situation and two ways of figuring each of two double track situations. The double track situations are two tracks with current of traffic operation and sidings, and two tracks with bi-directional operation and no sidings. The two methods of figuring are scheduled operation with transportation schedules and "strict priority" operation with transportation schedules. "Strict priority" operation means that no train may be delayed for a less important (less priority) train. The level of importance of the example trains is numerical order, with train 2 being most important and train 730 being least important (the 700 series trains are treated as equally unimportant, however).

The current situation is given for the single track example and for the two track examples. The live file is shown for each example, containing the latest lineups for Albany and Galveston as well as notes left as information develops and a note from the chief dispatcher with instructions for handling No. 730.

Each stage of planning (current situation, fresh figures, finding conflicts, and conflict resolution) is described on a page facing the trainsheet information being described (description on the left page, trainsheet on the right page). The same information is represented on a diagram on the next right page so that it is easy to compare the description to the trainsheet or the diagram.

The running times are simplified to facilitate the examples. Trains are figured the same way regardless of stops in any example or of crossing over in the two track examples.

WWD						EWD			
99*	717	715	101	5		2	68	712	730
1455	1400	1100	1030	1152	Albany	1155	1100	1215	1700
	30m	35m			Eugene			30m	30m
1640	1700	1400	1200	1259	Galveston	1048	0900	0900	1345

Fig. 15-3 Transportation schedules are generally not produced in timetable format. Each train has a separate page (or pages) representing the entire schedule of the train. One of the regularly assigned train dispatchers on a district may maintain a timetable format of the schedules for trains on the district, or at least the most important ones. Typical of transportation schedules, No 5 cannot leave on time if No 2 is on time (in the single track example) and No 712 cannot leave on time if No 68 is on time.

*No 99 operates only in the two track examples.

Westward			Train	Eastward		
700-799	50-199	1-10		1-10	50-199	700-799
		cf 1h	A Albany / 1h call			
20	15	10	B Boston	10	15	25
20	15	10	C Chicago	10	15	20
20	15 cf 1h	10	D Detroit	10	15	20 cf 1h5m
25 cf 1h10m	15	10	E Eugene	10	15 cf 1h	20
from arr 20	15	10	F Fargo	10	15	20
20	15	10	G Galveston / 1h call	10 cf 1h	15	20

Fig. 15-4 This crutch shows the running times used in all of the examples. A crutch is used as a training aid when a dispatcher is learning a district, so it shows typical running times for each type of train, the office call at each station (there is no more telegraph, but office calls are useful shorthand and are sometimes still used for that purpose), the length of call required at the terminals (both Albany and Galveston need a one hour call on each train), and the location of trains at typical running time when a call figure must be put out.

The planning examples section is "sideways", with the book turned so that the binding is up and the right edge is down. This allows larger illustrations so that the details may be shown clearly.

EXAMPLE 1 - SINGLE TRACK

The example for single track begins on the next page.

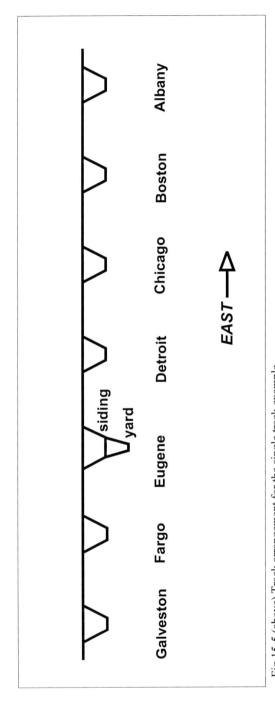

Galveston   Fargo   Eugene   Detroit   Chicago   Boston   Albany

siding
yard

EAST ⟶

Fig 15-5 (above) Track arrangement for the single track example.

Fig. 15-6 (below) Live file information for the single track example.

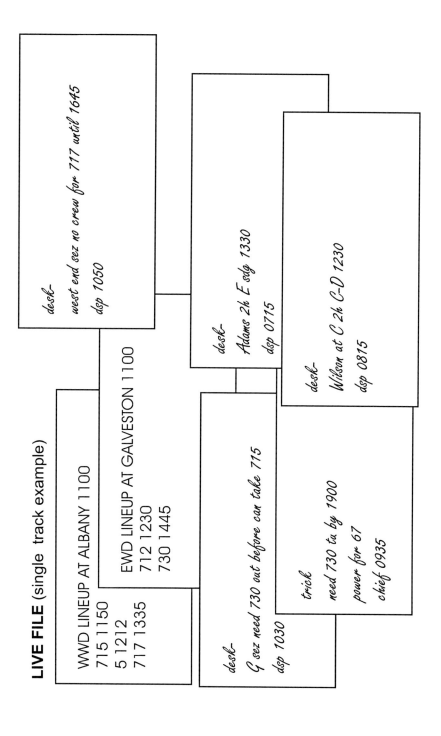

LIVE FILE (single track example)

WWD LINEUP AT ALBANY 1100
715 1150
5 1212
717 1335

EWD LINEUP AT GALVESTON 1100
712 1230
730 1445

desk-
west end sez no crew for 717 until 1645
dsp 1050

desk-
Adams 2h E sdg 1330
dsp 0715

desk-
Wilson at C 2h C-D 1230
dsp 0815

desk-
G sez need 730 out before can take 715
dsp 1030

trick
need 730 tu by 1900
power for 67
chief 0935

Fig. 15-7 The facing page shows the situation at 1110. No. 68 has arrived at Albany, 5 minutes late on its 1050 call figure (note that No. 68 could not maintain the running times shown in the crutch). No. 101 has just met No. 2 at Eugene and is called into Galveston for 1140. No. 2 is called into Albany for On Time.

Westward		Train	Eastward	
101	5		2	68
0950		Albany		1055
		Boston		
1020		Chicago		1020 / 1008
		Detroit		
1050 / 1110		Eugene	1108	0933
		Fargo	1058	0918
		Galveston	1048	0900

df 1050 · *df 07* · *df 1140*

Fig. 15-8 The diagram below represents the same information found on the trainsheet example on the previous page (Fig. 15-7).

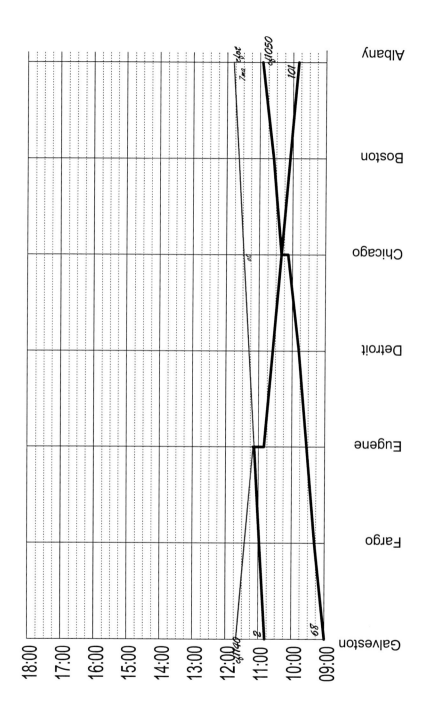

Fig. 15-9 The information to be used in planning has accumulated in the live file. Planning information may also be found on the trainsheet, left over from earlier planning or marked on the sheet as information is received. The chief left a note saying No. 730's power stands for No. 67 and must be tied up at Albany by 1900. At the beginning of the shift, two maintenance of way foremen gave their plans for the afternoon. Wilson needs 2 hours between Chicago and Detroit after 1230, planning to get on the track at Chicago. Adams needs the siding at Eugene at 1330 for 2 hours. At Galveston, the yard says No. 730 must get out before No. 715 can get in and the other side says there is no crew for No. 717 until 1645.

The next step is to pencil everything you know onto the trainsheet. Figure the time for each train without consideration for the others.

	Westward				Train	Eastward			
	717	715	101	5		2	68	712	730
Albany	1335	1150	0950	1212	Albany	1148	1055	1455	1720
	ot 1400			20ml		7ma		ot 1215	ot 1700
Boston					Boston				
Chicago	1415	1230	1080	1232	Chicago	1128	1020	1410	1635
					Wilson 1030 2h	ot	1008		
Detroit					Detroit				
Eugene	1500	1315	1050	1252	Eugene	1108	0933	1330	1555
	1530 pa 1600	1350 pa 1400	1110	20ml	Adams 1330 2h sdg	1058	0918	1310	1525
Fargo					Fargo				
Galveston	1610	1430	1140	1312	Galveston	1048	0900	1230	1445
	ot 1700	ot 1400	of 1140	13ml				ot 0900	ot 1345

crew 1645　730 oat 1st

Top notes: of 07　of 1050　61's pwer* by 1900

Fig. 15-10 The diagram below represents the same information found on the trainsheet example on the previous page (Fig. 15-9).

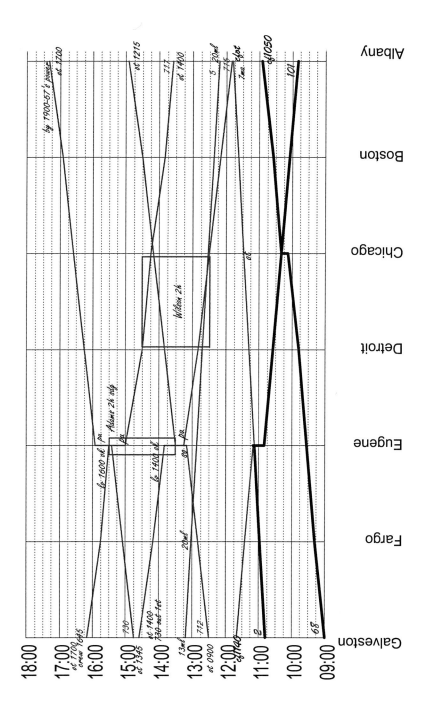

Fig. 15-11 Look for conflicts (trains or trains and track maintenance that would occupy the same track and location at the same time). Mark each one. Before moving on to another train, check to make sure that there is something on every train that will be encountered and all of the expected maintenance work.

There is nothing to do for No. 2. It will go to Albany for everybody. The situation is the same for No. 101.

No. 5 is the most important of the remaining trains. It is 20 minutes late at Albany, but allowed to make track speed can be 13 minutes late at Galveston.

No. 715 cannot make Chicago for No. 5, will pass Chicago at the time Wilson wants to begin work, will be at Eugene at the same time as No. 712 and during the time Adams wants to work on the siding, and cannot go beyond Fargo for No. 730. All of the conflicts for No. 715 have been identified.

No. 712 Cannot make Eugene for No. 5, will be working at Eugene at the same time as No. 712, will leave Detroit during the time Wilson wants to work between Chicago and Detroit, and will see No. 717 at Chicago. All of the conflicts for No. 712 have been identified.

No. 717 looks right now like it will be at Chicago for No. 712 and will be between Chicago and Detroit during the two hours Wilson wants to work. No. 717 will be at Eugene working at the same time as No. 730, which is also the same time that Adams wants to work on the siding. All of the conflicts for No. 717 have been identified.

No. 730 is already figured for No. 715 at Fargo and No. 717 at Eugene. No. 730 will also be at Eugene at the same time that Adams wants to work on the siding. All of the conflicts for No. 730 have been identified.

	Westward			Train	Eastward			
717	**715**	**101**	**5**		**2**	**68**	**712**	**730**
1335 / ot 1400	1150	0950	1212 / 20ml	Albany	1148 / 7ma		1455 / ot 1215	1720 / ot 1700
			20ml / (715)	Boston		1055		
1415 / (712)	1230	1020	1232	Chicago	1128 / ot	1020 / 1008 ot	1410 / 777	1635
		1050		Detroit Wilson 1330 2h				
1500 / 730 / 1530 pa 1600	1315 / 712 / 1350 pa 1400 / 730	1110	1252 / 20ml	Eugene Adams 1330 2h sig	1108	0933	1330 / 715 / 1310 so	1555 / 717 / 1525 pa
	730		712	Fargo	1058	0918	(5)	715
1610 / ot 1700	1430 / ot 1400	1140	1312 / 13ml	Galveston	1048	0900	1230 / ot 0900	1445 / ot 1345
crew 1645	730 / out 7et	of 1140			of 07	of 1050		61's power by 1900

Fig. 15-12 The diagram below represents the same information found on the trainsheet example on the previous page (Fig. 15-11).

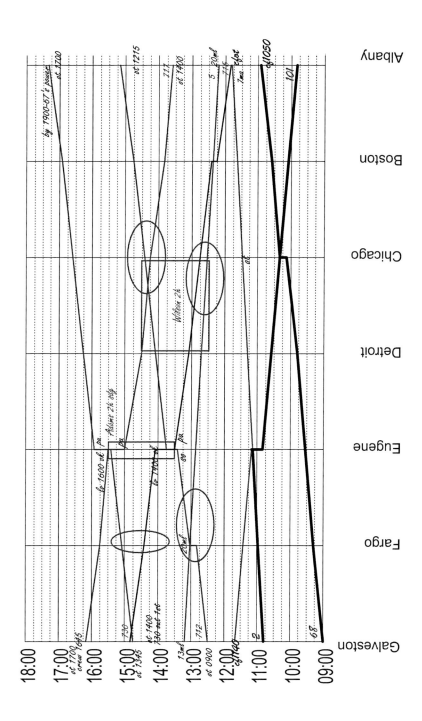

Fig. 15-13 Two hours on the siding at 1330 for Adams is not going to work. Lets see if we can get Adams on the radio. We'll ask if he can re-arrange his schedule and start at Eugene by 1130 and be out of there by 1330. There isn't a good alternative.

Adams says he can do that. To make this work, No. 712 needs to be able to pull through the yard to set out

Ask Adams if No. 712 will be able to make that move. He says there is only one clear track, but they can pull the setout into the yard and return on the siding. They will not be able to get back to their train until he's finished. He'll give it back as soon as he can. He's headed for Eugene in his truck now.

Tell Adams that's the plan; call when he gets to Eugene.

Go back to figuring.

It looks like No. 715 will be at Boston for No. 5. Left to run, No. 715 would have passed Chicago just as Wilson wanted to work between Chicago and Detroit. After following No. 5, it will be much later than that. No. 715 and

No. 712 will be at Eugene working at the same time while Adams is working on the siding, adding to the time No. 715 needs for the work at Eugene. No. 715 is later than originally figured, but can't go to Galveston for No. 730, so the probable Fargo meet with No. 730 has not changed. All of the conflicts for No. 715 have been identified.

It looks like No. 712 will be at Fargo for No. 5. No. 712 and No. 715 will be working at Eugene at the same time. No. 712 will also be there at the same time as Adams wants to work on the siding. It looks like No. 712 will meet No. 717 at Chicago. That involves running from Detroit to Chicago during the 2 hours that Wilson wants. All of the conflicts for No. 712 have been identified.

	Westward				Train	Eastward			
	717	715	101	5		2	68	712	730
Albany	1335 / ot 1400	1150	0950 / 20ml	1212	Albany	1148	1055 / 7ma	1510 / ot 1215	1720
Boston			1215 / (5) / 1225	(715) / 1222	Boston				ot 1700
Chicago	1415 / (712)	1245	1020	1232	Chicago	1128	1020	1425 / (717)	1635
Detroit					Wilson 1730 2h / Detroit	ot	1008		
Eugene	1500 / 730	1330 / (712)	1050	1252	Eugene	1108	0933	1345 / 715	1555 / 717
Fargo	1530 pa / 1600	1410 pa / 1400	1110	1302 / (712) / 20ml	Adams 1730 2h sdg / Fargo	1058	0918	1325 so / 715	1525 pa
		730		1302 / (712)		1048		(5) 1302 / 1255	(715)
Galveston	1610 / ot 1700	1455 / ot 1400	1140	1312 / 13ml	Galveston		0900	1230 / ot 0900	1445 / ot 1345

of 07 · of 1050 · 61's power by 1900

open 730 · out Tot 1645 · of 1140

Fig. 15-14 The diagram below represents the same information found on the trainsheet example on the previous page (Fig. 15-13).

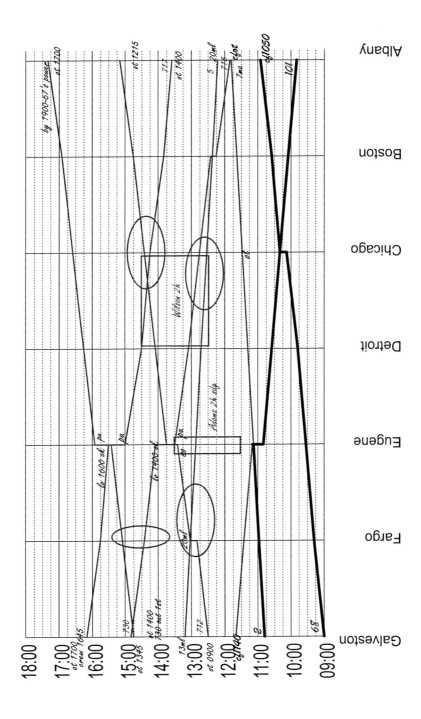

Fig. 15-15 No. 715 and No. 712 will see No. 5 before they get to Eugene. Figure the time No. 5 will let each of them out and figure the rest of the trip for each.

Adams will be finished at Eugene before No. 717 and No. 730 show up, so those marks can be erased.

No. 712 and No. 715 are of equal importance. Both are irretrievably late. The "best meet" is appropriate for them. No. 712 will cut off west of Eugene, pull the train into the yard and wait for Adams to finish before returning to the train. Adams will be finished by the time they are in the clear in the yard, but making the move this way instead of pulling to the east switch and backing the cars in will take an extra 10 minutes. No. 712 will not let No. 715 out of the west end of Eugene to make the pickup until 1345. No. 715's work will take 15 minutes more than originally figured. No. 715 will be at Fargo for No. 730. That doesn't look like it will change, so figure the time out of Fargo and into Galveston.

No. 5 lets No. 712 out of Fargo at 1302. No. 712 is at Eugene from 1325 until 1355 to set out and wait for Adams to give the siding back. That puts No. 712 by Chicago at 1435 and into Albany at 1520.

No. 5 lets No. 715 out of Boston at 1225. That puts No. 715 by Chicago at 1245 and into Eugene at 1330. No. 715 will be hung by No. 712's rear end east of Eugene and won't get out of Eugene until 1420. No. 730 will let No. 715 out of Fargo at 1505. That puts No. 715 into Galveston at 1525.

Change the pencil marks on the sheet for these new figures.

Westward				Train	Eastward			
717	715	101	5		2	68	712	717
					of 07	*of 1050*		*61's power by 1900*
1335	1150	0950	1212	Albany	1148	1055	1520	1720
at 1400			20ml		7ma		at 1215	at 1700
								730
	1215/⑤ 1225		715 (circle) 1222	Boston				
1415 ⑦⑫	1245	1020	1232	Chicago	1128 / ot	1020	1435 ⑦⑰	1635
				Wilson 1030 2h Detroit		1008		
1500-730	1330-712	1050	1252	Eugene	1108	0933	1355 ⑦⑮	1555-717
1530 pa 1600	1410 pa 1400 / 1430-730 / 1505	1110	20ml	Adams 1130 2h sdg			715 / 1325 so	1525 pa / 715
			1302-712 / 1312	Fargo	1058	0918	⑤ 1302 / 1255	715 / 1505
			13ml					
1610	1525	1140		Galveston	1048	0900	1230	1445
at 1700	at 1400						ot 0900	ot 1345
crew 1645	730 / ot 1st	of 1140						

Fig. 15-16 The diagram below represents the same information found on the trainsheet example on the previous page (Fig. 15-15).

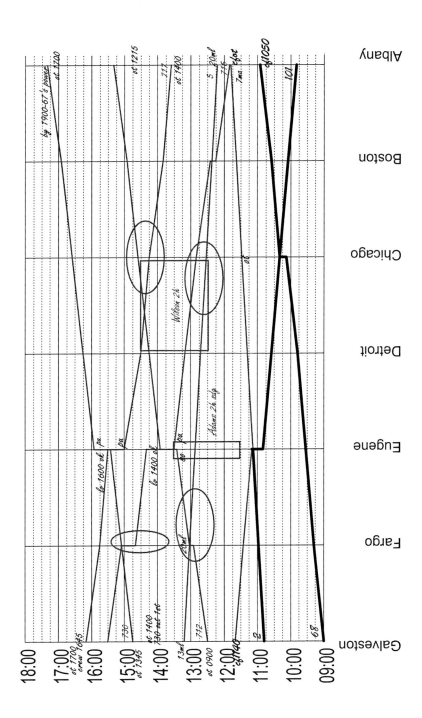

Fig. 15-17 No. 712 won't let No. 717 out of Chicago until 1435. That puts No. 717 at Eugene from 1525 until 1555 and into Galveston at 1635. No. 717 and No. 730 will be working at Eugene at the same time; one on the siding and the other on the main.

Train	Westward					Eastward			
	717	715	101	5		2	68	712	730
Albany	1335 / ot 1400	1150	0950	1212 / 20ml		1148	1055	1520 / ot 1215	1720 / ot 1700
Boston		1215 / 1225 (5)		(715) / 1222		7ma			
Chicago	1415 / 1435 (712)	1245	**1020**	1232		1128 ot	1020	1435 (717)	1635
Detroit (Wilson 1230 2k)							1008		1615
Eugene (Adams 1130 2k sdg)	1525 (730) / 1555 pa	1330 (712) / 1410 pa 1600	1050	1252 / 20ml		**1108**	**0933**	1355 (715) / 1325 so	1555 (717) / 1525 pa
Fargo	1555 pa	1430 (730) / 1505	1110	1302 (712)		**1058**	**0918**	(5) 1302 / 1255	715 / 1505
Galveston	1635 / ot 1700	1525 / ot 1400	1140	1312 / 13ml		1048	0900	1230 / ot 0900	1445 / ot 1345

Westward annotations: crew 730, 1645 out 1st, of 1140

Eastward annotations: of 07, of 1050, 61's power by 1900

Fig. 15-18 The diagram below represents the same information found on the trainsheet example on the previous page (Fig. 15-17).

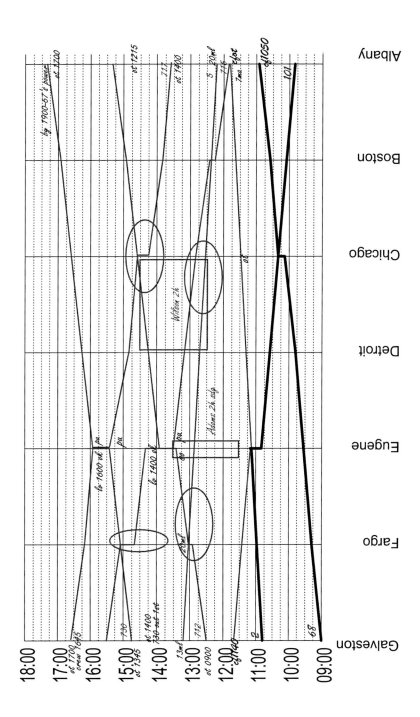

Fig. 15-19 The only conflicts left are No. 715, No. 712, No. 717 and No. 730 against the time that Wilson wants between Chicago and Detroit. Letting him go to work right behind No. 5 will have No. 715 at Chicago for him, No. 717 behind No. 715, and No. 712 at Detroit for him. The delays would be very large and the congestion at Eugene would last until after 1715.

If Wilson is given his two hours between Chicago and Detroit right after No. 717 leaves Chicago, No. 730 will be at Detroit until 1635 and will get into Albany at 1755. Before talking to Wilson, it's time to talk to the yard at Albany and find out what an hour late on No. 730 will do.

The yardmaster says that the car inspectors will not finish working No. 712 until at least 1830 so he doesn't need No. 730 until 1900 (the same time the Chief needs the power).

It's time to call Wilson on the radio and tell him that he will not get the track between Chicago and Detroit until after No. 717 leaves Chicago at 1435.

Starting that late will mean that Wilson will be on overtime before finishing. Wilson says that this work must be done today and his supervisor wants him to work overtime if necessary to finish. He has a project he can finish in the yard at Chicago first and can be in position to leave Chicago right behind No. 717. He will clear up at a road crossing near the work location by 1645.

The only thing left to do is publish it, make it happen, and watch carefully for changes in the situation.

Westward				Train	Eastward			
717	715	101	5		2	68	712	730
1335 ot 1400	1150	0950	1212 20ml	Albany	1148	1055 7ma	1520 ot 1215	1755 ot 1700
	1215 (5) 1225		715 1222	Boston				
1415 1435 712	1245	1020	1232	Chicago	1128 ot	1020 1008	1435	1710
				Wilson 135 2h10m Detroit			717	1645 1615
1525 730 1555 pa	1330 712 1410 pa 1400	1050 1110	1252 20ml	Eugene Adams 1130 2h sdg	1108	0933	1355 715 1325 sv	1555 717 1525 pa
	1430 730 1505		712 1302 1312 13ml	Fargo	1058	0918	1302 (5) 1255	715 1505
1635 ot 1700	1525	1140		Galveston	1048	0900	1230 ot 0900	1445 ot 1345

crew 730 1645
out Tot 1400
of 1140

yd rdy 1830 · 61's power by 1900 · of 1050 · of 07

Fig. 15-20 The diagram below represents the same information found on the trainsheet example on the previous page (Fig. 15-19).

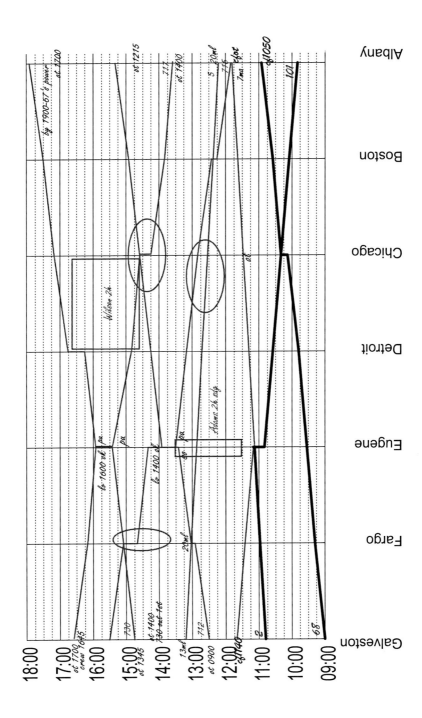

When watching for changes that affect the plan, some are important; others are not.

No. 715 only has 5 minutes to spare at Boston. This needs to be watched closely as No. 715 approaches Albany on the other side. Talk to the other side and explain the move. If the other side decides to put No. 715 in for No. 2 east of Albany it is time to refigure.

If No. 2 has a problem west of Albany and doesn't let No. 715 out by 1154, it all falls apart.

No. 712 can only fall down 4 minutes before it gets into No. 5. Talk to the other side and explain the move. If No. 712 can't leave Galveston for No. 5, it is time to refigure.

No. 717 can lose 20 minutes before anything changes, since they will be at Chicago 20 minutes for No. 712. No. 717 can lose 50 minutes before the change affects No. 730. Tell the yard at Albany or the other side about the 20 minutes available that will not change the plan.

Any change in No. 730 requires refiguring No. 715 for a call figure, but that's all.

Example 2 - Two Tracks, Current of Traffic, and Sidings

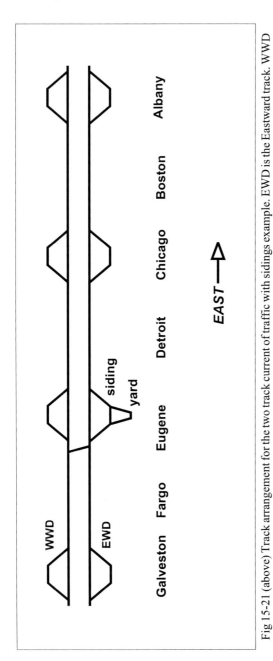

Fig 15-21 (above) Track arrangement for the two track current of traffic with sidings example. EWD is the Eastward track. WWD is the westward track.

Fig. 15-22 (below) Live file information for the two track current of traffic with sidings example.

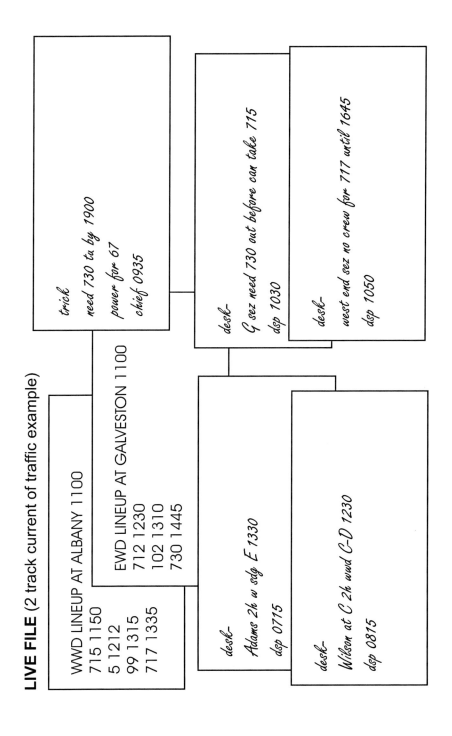

LIVE FILE (2 track current of traffic example)

WWD LINEUP AT ALBANY 1100
715 1150
5 1212
99 1315
717 1335

EWD LINEUP AT GALVESTON 1100
712 1230
102 1310
730 1445

trick
need 730 ta by 1900
power for 67
chief 0935

desk-
G sez need 730 out before can take 715
dsp 1030

desk-
west end sez no crew for 717 until 1645
dsp 1050

desk-
Adams 2h w sdg E 1330
dsp 0715

desk-
Wilson at C 2h wwd C-D 1230
dsp 0815

Fig. 15-23 The facing page shows the situation at 1110. No. 68 has arrived at Albany (five minutes late on the call figure, losing running time throughout the trip). No. 101 is called into Galveston for 1120 and No. 2 is called into Albany for On Time.

	Westward		Train	Eastward	
	101	5		2	68
				of 07	*of 1045*
Albany	0950				1050
Boston					
Chicago	1020				1008
Detroit					
Eugene	1050			1108	0933
Fargo					
Galveston				1048	0900

of 1120

Fig. 15-24 The diagram below represents the same information found on the trainsheet example on the previous page (Fig. 15-23).

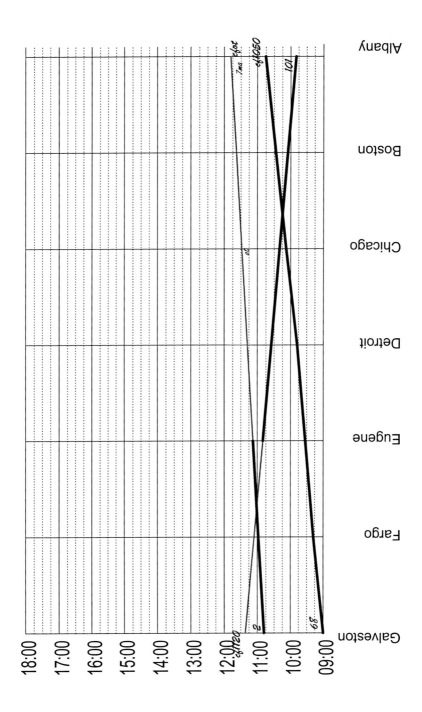

Fig. 15-25 Pencil everything you know (live file information; conversations with the chief, yardmasters, maintenance of way personnel, the dispatchers on the other side, and others; and any other available information) on the trainsheet.

	Westward				Train			Eastward		
717	715	99	101	5		2	68	102	712	730
						of 07	*of 1045*			*67's pwr by 1900*
1335	1150	OT 1455 / 1315	0950	20ml / 1212	Albany	1148	1050	OT1645 / 1440	OT1215 / 1455	OT1700 / 1720
					Boston	7ma				
1415	1230	1345	1020	1232	Chicago	1128	1008	1410	1410	1635
					Wilson 1230 Detroit 2h wwdb					
1500 1600 ob / 1530 pa	1315 1400 ob / 1350 pa	1415	1050	1252 / 20ml	Eugene Adams 1330 2h wwdg	1108	0933	1340	1330 / 1310 so	1555 / 1525 pa
					Fargo	1048				
1610	1430	1445		1312	Galveston		0900	1310	1230	1445
OT1700	OT1400	OT1640		13ml				OT1500		

crew 1645   730   out 1st   of 1120

Fig. 15-26 The diagram below represents the same information found on the trainsheet example on the previous page (Fig. 15-25).

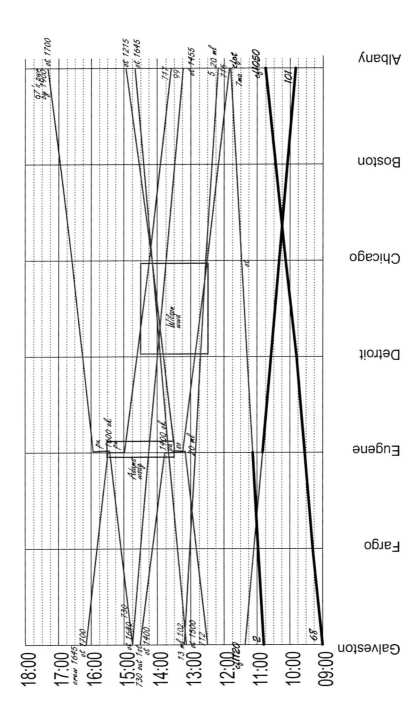

TRANSPORTATION SCHEDULE OPERATION

Fig. 15-27 Look for conflicts. Mark each one. Before moving on to another train, check to make sure that there is something on every train that will be encountered and on all of the expected maintenance work.

There is nothing to do for No. 2. It will go to Albany for everybody. The situation is the same for No. 101. No. 5 is the most important of the remaining trains. It is twenty minutes late at Albany, allowed to make track speed, can be thirteen minutes late at Galveston.

No. 715 cannot make Chicago for No. 5, so No. 715 will be at Albany. This puts No. 715 at Galveston at 1450, five minutes after No. 730 is due to leave. 1450, however, is five minutes after No. 99 will arrive at Galveston. No. 715 could remain in the westward siding at Eugene for No. 99, but the additional delay is not necessary since No. 99 will still arrive at Galveston one hour forty five minutes early.

	Westward					Train				Eastward		67's pwr by 1900
717	715	99	101	5			of 07 2	of 1045 68	102	712	730	
1335	1150 / 1215 (5)	OT 1455 / 1315	0950	20ml / 1212 (715)		Albany	1148 / 7ma	1050	OT1645 / 1440	OT1215 / 1455	OT1700 / 1720	
						Boston						
1415	1255	1345	1020	1232		Chicago	1128	1008	1410 / (712)	1410 / (102)	1635	
						Wilson 1230 Detroit 2h wait						
1500 / 1000 ak / 1530 pa	1335 / 100 ak / 1410 pa	1415	1050	1252 / 20ml		Eugene Adams 1330 2h usdg	1108 / 0933	0933	1340	1330 / 1310 so	1555 / 1525 pa	
						Fargo						
1610	1450	1455 / (715/730)	1120	1312		Galveston	1048	0900	1310	1230	1445	
OT1700	OT1400	OT1640	of 1120	13ml					OT1500			

crew 1645 730 out 1st (99)

Fig. 15-28 The diagram below represents the same information found on the trainsheet example on the previous page (Fig. 15-27).

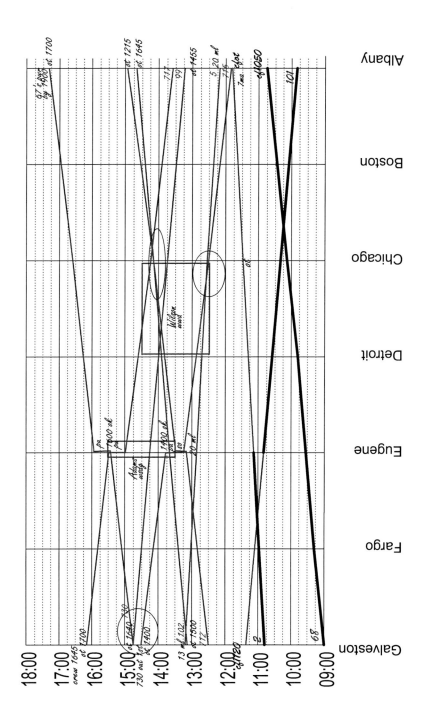

Fig. 15-29 Wilson and Adams must be considered. Maintenance of way forces go to work at 0700 and the workday is finished at 1600. It appears that Wilson must wait for No. 99. He can go to work 1345 and be finished at 1545. If he does so, No. 717 cannot leave Chicago until 1545 and will not arrive at Galveston until 1740 (48 minutes late), after starting the trip 25 minutes ahead. Adams needs the westward siding at Eugene for two hours after 1330. Since No. 99 will be left to follow No. 715 into Galveston, No. 717 can hold the westward main track at Eugene, allowing Adams to go to work at 1330. Adams will be finished before No. 717 arrives.

No. 99, following No. 715 from Eugene, can be one hour 45 minutes ahead at Galveston. If Wilson is allowed to go to work at 1255 right behind No. 715, No. 99 can leave Chicago at 1455 and arrive at Galveston at 1555 (45 minutes ahead). No. 717 would then leave Chicago at 1500 behind No. 99 and would arrive at Galveston at 1650 (five minutes after the crew is available and ten minutes ahead on the schedule). Change Wilson's start time on the sheet to 1255, change the figures for No. 99 and No. 717, and

tell Wilson about the change. He may be able to use the time for minor tasks he planned for later in the day.

The situation is the same between No. 102 and No. 712. No. 712 can be held at Eugene for 10 minutes for No. 102, allowing No. 102 to arrive at Albany at 1440 (two hours fifty minutes ahead), or can stay ahead to Albany allowing No. 102 to arrive at 1500 (one hour 45 minutes ahead). Change No. 102's figures to show following No. 712.

	Westward					Train	Eastward				
	717	715	99	101	5		2	68	102	712	730
Albany	1335	1150 / 1215 (5)	OT 1455 / 1315	0950	20ml / 1212 (715)	Albany	1148 / 7ma	1050	OT1645 / 1500	OT1215 / 1455	OT1700 / 1720
Boston						Boston					
Chicago	1415 / 1500	1255	1345 / 1455	1020	1232	Chicago	1128	1008	1415 / 712	1410 / 102	1635
Detroit						Wilson Detroit 2h wait 1255					
Eugene	1540 1600 pa / 1335 1410 pa		1525	1050	1252 / 20ml	Eugene Adams 1330 2h wsdp	1108	0933	1340	1330 / 1310 so	1555 / 1525 pa
Fargo						Fargo					
Galveston	1650	1450	1555	1120	1312 / 13ml	Galveston	1048	0900	1310	1230	1445
	crew 1645 / OT1700	OT1400	OT1640	of 1120		730 out 1st			OT1500		

of 07   of 1045   67's pwr by 1900

Fig. 15-30 The diagram below represents the same information found on the trainsheet example on the previous page (Fig. 15-29).

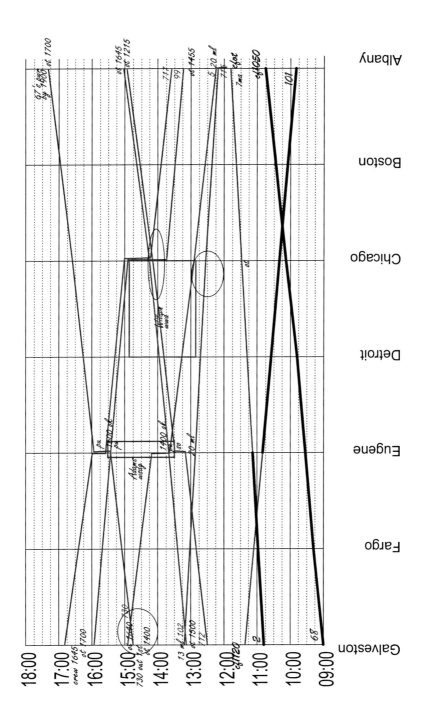

"STRICT PRIORITY" OPERATION

Fig. 15-31 No. 99 is a high priority train. It must not be delayed for lower priority trains.

If No. 715 leaves Eugene ahead of No. 99, No. 99 will be delayed 5 minutes, which is contrary to the train handling instructions. No. 715 will follow No.99 from Eugene, waiting thirty-five minutes for No. 99. Adams cannot have the westward siding at Eugene until 1420. The work requires two hours, or until 1620, but since the workday ends at 1600 (unless Adams' supervisor decides that it is worthwhile to do the work on overtime). Tell Adams that he cannot have the westward siding at Eugene until 1420. He says he'll try tomorrow. Pencil the new figures on the sheet (and cross out or erase the time Adams wanted) and continue planning. No. 99 will arrive at Galveston 1 hour fifty-five minutes ahead.

Wilson cannot begin work between Chicago and Detroit until No. 99 passes at 1345. He can complete the work by 1545 and (assuming that the work is close to his headquarters) finish during the normal workday. If Wilson is allowed to do the work, No. 717 will be delayed one hour thirty minutes. Since No. 717 is not a priority train and there are no handling instructions to the contrary, Wilson can go to work following No. 99. No. 717 will arrive at Galveston at 1740, 40 minutes late.

No. 102 will be on No. 712's block coming into Chicago. Since No. 102 is higher priority, No. 712 must stay at Eugene for No. 102, waiting five minutes. No. 102 will arrive at Albany two hours five minutes ahead.

	Eastward					Train		Westward			
730	**712**	**102**	**68** *of 1050*	**2** *of 07*		**5**	**101**	**99**	**715**	**717**	
OT1700	OT1215	OT1645		*1148* 7ma	Albany	1212 20ml	*0950*	OT1455	1150	1335	
1720	1510	1440	*1045*		Boston			1315	1215		
1635	1425	1410		*1128*	Chicago	1232	*1020*	1345	1255	1545	
			1008		Detroit — Wilson 1345, 2h wait						
1555	1345	1340	*0933*	*1108*	Eugene — Adams 1330 2h rustg	1252 20ml	*1050*	1415	1340 ob / 1420 pa	1630 / 1600 ob / 1700 pa	
1525 pa	1310 so		*0918*	*1058*	Fargo	1312 13ml					
1445	1230	1310	*0900*	*1048*	Galveston			1445	1505	1740	
by 1900		OT1500				of 1120		OT1640	OT1400	OT1700	

67's pwr by 1900

crew 730 out 1st
1645

Fig. 15-32 The diagram below represents the same information found on the trainsheet example on the previous page (Fig. 15-31).

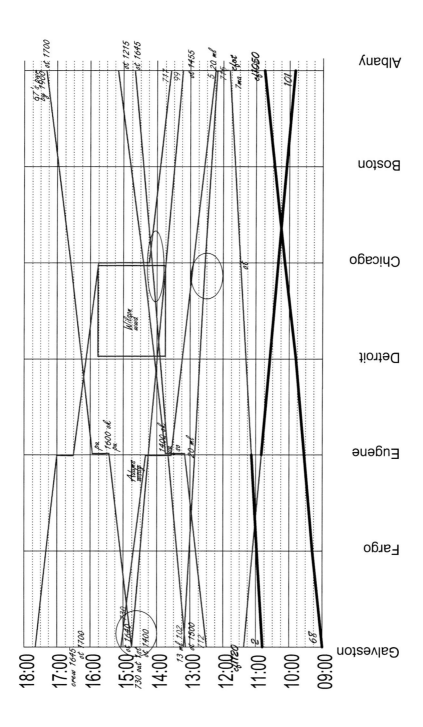

Example 3 - Two Tracks, Bi-directional Signaling, No Sidings

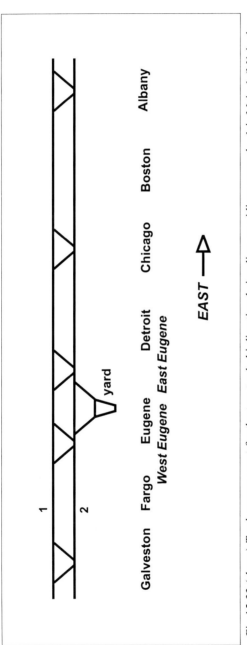

Fig 15-33 (above) Track arrangement for the two track, bi-directional signaling, no sidings example. 1 is Main 1 (M1 in the discussion), 2 is Main 2 (M2 in the discussion).

Fig. 15-34 (below) Live file information for the two track, bi-directional signaling, no sidings example.

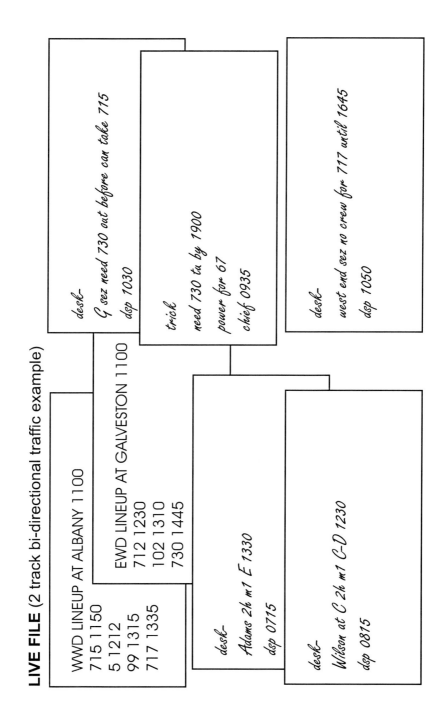

LIVE FILE (2 track bi-directional traffic example)

WWD LINEUP AT ALBANY 1100
715 1150
5 1212
99 1315
717 1335

EWD LINEUP AT GALVESTON 1100
712 1230
102 1310
730 1445

desk–
G sez need 730 out before can take 715
dsp 1030

trick
need 730 ta by 1900
power for 67
chief 0935

desk–
west end sez no crew for 717 until 1645
dsp 1050

desk–
Adams 2k m1 E 1330
dsp 0715

desk–
Wilson at C 2k m1 C-D 1230
dsp 0815

Pencil everything you know (live file information; conversations with the chief dispatcher, yardmasters, maintenance of way personnel, and train dispatchers on the other side; and any other available information).

TRANSPORTATION SCHEDULE OPERATION

Fig. 15-35 The two track, bi-directional signaling in this example provides opportunities for greater creativity, however it also makes evaluation of the plan a more complex process. On a single track line, the only movement opportunities are on the main track and sidings. There is always potential conflict between opposing trains. On a two track current of traffic line, the only movement opportunities are generally the main track with the current of traffic and the sidings. There is no potential conflict between opposing trains. (There is an exception for a two track current of traffic line that is arranged for normal movements against the current of traffic on written authority. Planning for this arrangement is the same as planning for a two track line with bi-directional signaling.)

On a two track bi-directional signaled line, the movement opportunities for any train can occur on any main track (and on sidings if there are any). All opposing and following movements have potential conflicts that must be examined while planning. The procedure is otherwise the same as for single track or two track current of traffic planning.

Westward / Eastward

cf 07 (over 2) · cf 1050 (over 68) · 67's pwr by 1900 (over 730)

717	715	99	101	5	Train	2	68	102	712	730
		OT 1455		20ml	Albany	1148		OT1645	OT1215	OT1700
1335	1150	1315	0950	1212		7ma	1045	1440	1455	1720
					Boston					
			1020		Chicago	1128	1008	1410	1410	1635
1415	1230	1345		1232						
					Wilson 1230 Detroit					
					2h m1					
1500 1600 ok	1315 1400 ok		1050	1252	Eugene	1108	0933	1340	1330	1555
1530 pu	1350 pu	1415		20ml	Adams 1330 2h m1				1310 so	1525 pu
					Fargo					
1610	1430	1445		1312	Galveston	1048	0900	1310	1230	1445
OT1700	OT1400			13ml						

crew 1645 (under 717) · 730 out 1st (under 715) · OT1640 (under 99) · cf 1120 (under 101) · OT1500 (under 102)

Fig. 15-36 The diagram below represents the same information found on the trainsheet example on the previous page (Fig. 15-35).

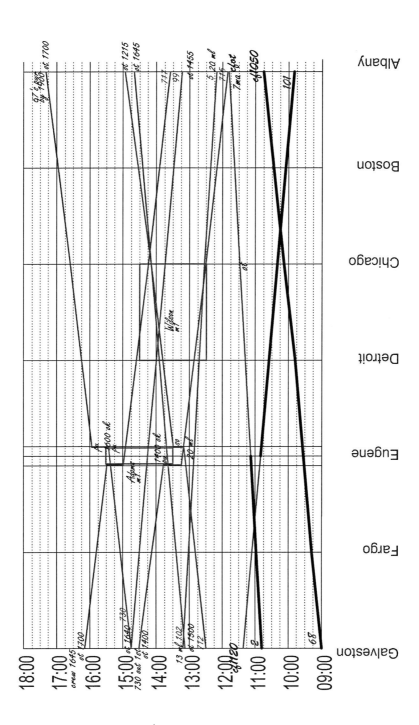

Fig. 15-37 There is no current of traffic, but there should be a normal flow of traffic (trains normally keep to the right or to the left). Look for conflicts. Mark each one. Begin by considering the normal flow of traffic to be the current of traffic, eliminating the need to look for conflicts between opposing trains. Before moving to another train, check to make sure that there is something on every train that will be encountered and on all of the expected maintenance work.

There is nothing to do for No. 2 and No. 101. No. 5 is the most important of the remaining trains. It is twenty minute late, but can be thirteen minutes late at Galveston if allowed to make track speed. No. 715 cannot leave Albany ahead of No. 5 on Main 1. No. 99 will overtake No. 715 between Fargo and Galveston while No. 715 is waiting for No. 730 to leave. No. 102 will overtake No. 712 just west of Chicago. Every conflict has been marked for every train.

	Westward					Train	of 07	of 1050		Eastward		67 & pwr by 1900
717	715	99	101	5			2	68	102	712	730
1335	1150	OT 1455 / 1315	0950	20ml / 1212		Albany	1148 / 7ma	1045	OT1645 / 1440	OT1215 / 1455	OT1700 / 1720
	(5)			(715)		Boston					
1415	1230	1345	1020	1232		Chicago	1128	1008	1410 / (712)	1410 / (102)	1635
						Wilson 1230 Detroit 26 m1					
1500 / 1600 ok / 1630 pa	1315 / 1350 pa	1415	1050	1252 / 20ml		Eugene Adams 1330 26 m1	1108	0933	1340	1330 / 1310 so	1555 / 1525 pa
						Fargo					
1610 / OT1700	1430 / OT1400	1445 / (715/730)		1312 / 13ml		Galveston	1048	0900	1310	1230	1445
crew 1645	730 out 1st (99)	OT1640	of 1120						OT1500		

Fig. 15-38 The diagram below represents the same information found on the trainsheet example on the previous page (Fig. 15-37).

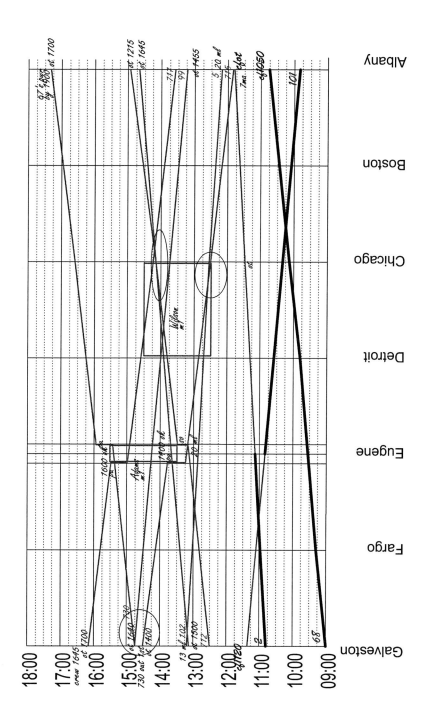

Fig. 15-39 Examine the possibility of No. 715 leaving Albany ahead of No. 5 by using Main 2 between Albany and Chicago. Looking at the eastward side of the sheet, No. 68 is in, No. 2 will be in at 1148, and the next train due at Albany that would be using Main 2 is number 102 figured for 1440 and not due until 1645. No. 102 will not leave Chicago until 1410. No. 712 is figured into Albany behind No. 102, but can pass Chicago at the same time as No. 102's figure. No. 715 can run on the reverse (Main 2) from Albany to Chicago, but would wait at Chicago for No. 5. It could continue to Eugene without a conflict, letting No. 5 pass on Main 1 without delay to either train. No. 715 can arrive at Eugene at 1315 and the first eastward train to leave is No. 102 at 1340.

Mark the figures on the sheet. The "]" symbol in No. 715's column is a typical trainsheet symbol for movement against the current of traffic or against the flow of traffic if the line has bi-directional signaling. (OSes for trains moving against the current of traffic are often written in red ink, however.) On a diagram, movement against the current or flow of traffic is often represented by color. For the examples, movement against the flow of traffic is represented by a broken line.

	Eastward					Train	Westward				
	2 *of 07*	**68** *of 1050*	**102**	**712**	**730** *67's pwr by 1900*		**5**	**101**	**99**	**715**	**717**
Albany	1148 7ma	1045	OT1645 1440	OT1215 1455	OT1700 1720		20ml 1212	0950	OT1455 1315	1150	1335
Boston											
Chicago	1128	1008	1410 (712)	1410 (102)	1635		1232	1020	1345	1230	1415
Detroit						Wilson 1230 2h m1					
Eugene	H08	0933	1340 (715)	1330 (715) 1310 so	1555 1525 pa	Adams 1330 2h m1	1252 20ml	1050	1415	1315 1600 ob 1350 pa	1500 1600 ob 1530 pa 102/712
Fargo											
Galveston	1048	0900	1310	1230	1445		1312 13ml		1445 715/730	1430 OT1400	1610 OT1700
					OT1500			of 1120	OT1640	730 out 1st (99)	crew 1645

Fig. 15-40 The diagram below represents the same information found on the trainsheet example on the previous page (Fig. 15-39).

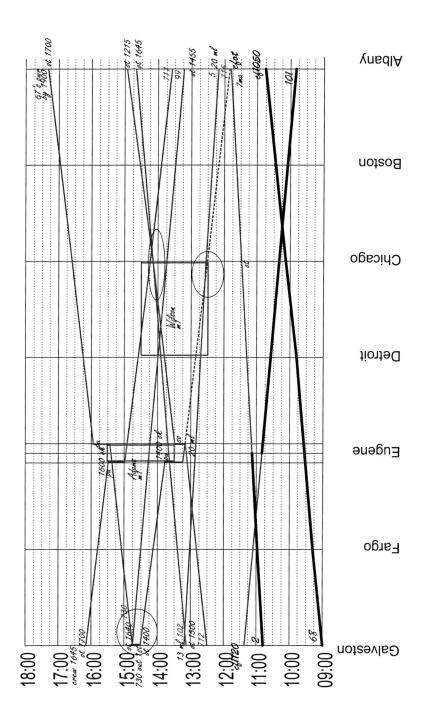

Fig. 15-41 The crossovers at both ends of Eugene allow great flexibility in the way that traffic is arranged, thus offering some alternatives that may allow Adams his two hours on Main 1. No. 715 will be working at Eugene from 1315 until 1350. Adams wants Main 1 at Eugene for two hours after 1330. No. 102 will pass Eugene at 1340, and No. 712 will be at Eugene between 1310 and 1330.

Before determining what track No. 715 should use at Eugene, it is necessary to determine how the other traffic must use the tracks. The figures for No. 715, No. 102, and No. 712 have them all at Eugene simultaneously. Adams will be waiting for train traffic, so the train traffic should be figured first.

No. 712 can leave at 1330 and arrive at Albany at 1455 (two hours thirty-five minutes late). If No. 102 is left to follow No. 712, it will be on No. 712's block from west of Chicago to Albany and arrive at Albany at 1500 (one hour forty-five minutes ahead). If No. 102 follows No. 712 from Eugene, the track used by both trains will be clear at 1340. By having No. 715 use Main 2 at Eugene for the pickup, Main 1 can be available to Adams ten minutes earlier. No. 712 will use Main 1 for the set out and No. 102

will follow through Eugene on Main 1 then on Main 2 from Eugene. Adams can go work on Main 1 at 1340 and be finished by 1540. Mark these figures on the sheet and continue planning.

	Westward					Train			Eastward		
	717	715	99	101	5		2	68	102	712	730
			OT 1455						OT1645	OT1215	OT1700
	1335	1150	1315	0950	20ml 1212	Albany	1148 7ma	1045	1500	1455	1720
						Boston					
	1415	1230	1345	1020	1232	Chicago	1128	1008	1415 (712)	1410 (102)	1635
						Wilson 1230 Detroit 2h mt					
	1500 1600 ok 1630 pa	1315 1600 ok 1350 pa	1415	1050	1252 20ml	Eugene Adams 1340 2h mt	1108	0933	1340 (715)	1330 715 / 1310 so	1555 / 1525 pa
	102/712					Fargo					
	1610 OT1700	1430 OT1400	1445 715/730		1312 13ml	Galveston	1048	0900	1310	1230	1445

cf 07 — 2 — cf 1050 — 68 — 67's pwr by 1900

crew 1645 — 730 — out 1st — (99) — OT1640 — cf 1120 — OT1500

Fig. 15-42 The diagram below represents the same information found on the trainsheet example on the previous page (Fig. 15-41).

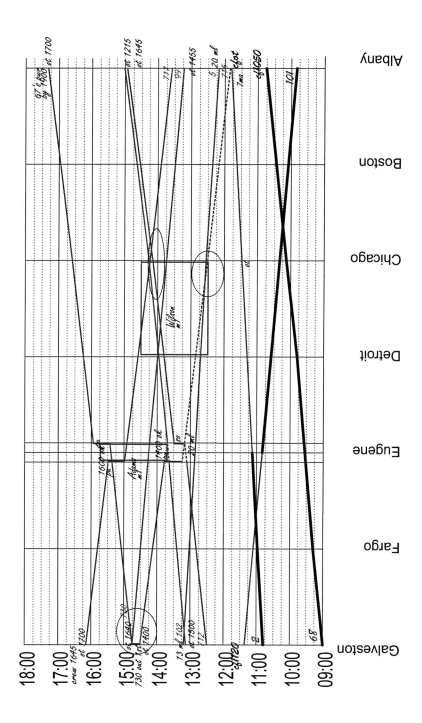

Fig. 15-43 Left to run on the figured times, No. 99 will stop behind No. 715 east of Galveston, waiting for No. 730 to leave. No. 101 would arrive one hour fifty minutes ahead of the schedule. Main 2 will have no eastward traffic at the time No. 99 is figured, so Adams can continue working and No. 99 can use Main 2 between East Eugene and West Eugene. No. 99 would meet No. 712 and No. 102 between Chicago and Eugene. Since both tracks would be required for the traffic, Wilson cannot have Main 1 until No. 99 has passed Chicago.

If Wilson is allowed to work on Main 1 between Chicago and Detroit immediately behind No. 5, he will be finished at 1430. If he waits for No. 99, he will not finish until 1545. Since No. 99 will arrive at Galveston one hour fifty minutes ahead after waiting behind No. 715 east of Galveston, there appears to be a way to allow Wilson to go to work. No. 102 and No. 712 will both be by Chicago on Main 2 at 1415, so No. 99 may be handled on the reverse from Chicago West Eugene, then regular from West Eugene to Galveston. After waiting for No. 712 and No. 102, No. 99 will arrive Galveston at 1515 (one hour twenty-five minutes ahead). Wilson can go to work behind No. 5 and will be finished at 1430.

of 07 *of 1050* *67's pwr by 1900*

	Westward				Train	Eastward				
717	**715**	**99**	**101**	**5**		**2**	**68**	**102**	**712**	**730**
1335	1150	OT 1455 / 1315	**0950**	20ml / 1212	Albany	1148	**1045** / 7ma	OT1645	OT1215	OT1700 / 1720
					Boston			1500	1455	
1415 / 1230	1230	1345 / 1415	**1020**	1232	Chicago	1128	**1008**	1415	1410	1635
		712/102			Wilson 1230 / Detroit 2h m1			715	1330 (715)	
1500 1600 ak / 1530 pa	1375 1400 ak / 1350 pa	1445	**1050**	1252 / 20ml	Eugene / Adams 1340 2h m1	**1108**	**0933**	1340	1310 so	1555 / 1525 pa
	102/712				Fargo	1048				
1610	1430	1515		1312 / 13ml	Galveston		0900	1310	1230	1445
OT1700	OT1400	OT1640						OT1500		

crew 1645 *730 out 1st* *of 1120*

Fig. 15-44 The diagram below represents the same information found on the trainsheet example on the previous page (Fig. 15-43).

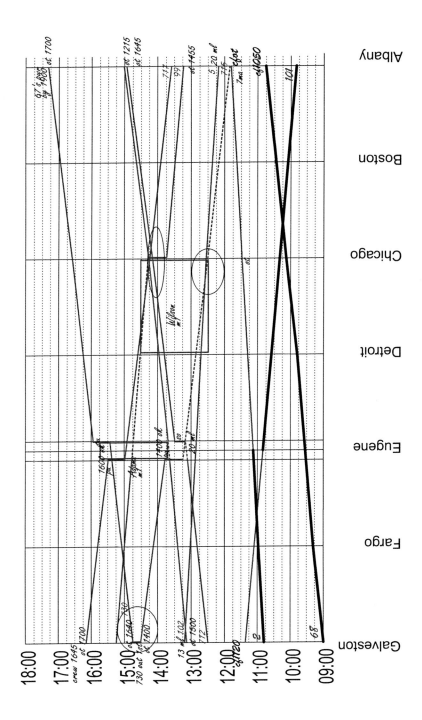

Fig. 15-45 The last remaining conflicts are No. 717 and Wilson on Main 1 between Chicago and Eugene, and No. 717 with Adams and No. 730 at Eugene. No. 717 will arrive Eugene at 1505. Left to go to work immediately, No. 717 will leave at 1535. No. 730 will arrive at 1525. Left to go to work immediately, No. 730 will leave at 1555.

Adams is working on Main 1 until 1540. If No. 717 pulls to the west end of Eugene on Main 2 to work on arrival, No. 730 will be delayed until No. 717 leaves at 1535. If No. 730 is left to go to work on Main 2 on arrival, then No. 717 will be delayed from 1505 until 1540 waiting for Adams. No. 730 is late. No. 717 is ahead on its schedule and can still arrive at Galveston ahead after waiting for Adams. There may be faster way to make his move.

It appears that it might be practical to reverse No. 717 from Chicago to Eugene behind No. 99 (rather than wait for Wilson to give Main 1 back) and cut off at East Eugene to hold the pickup (Fig. 15-53 page 166). No. 717 can run to the west end of the yard on Main 2 back into the yard, and shove the pickup back to the train east of East Eugene on Main 1. This move itself will take some extra time. Additional time may also be needed because both trains

are working the east end of Eugene yard simultaneously. This movement is being arranged to prevent delay to No. 730. If both trains are ready to use the east lead at Eugene, holding No. 730 for No. 717 would not be reasonable. No. 717 will leave Eugene at 1550 and arrive at Galveston before the connecting crew is rested (also 30 minutes ahead on the schedule). No. 730 will not be delayed by making the movement in this way.

There is a possibility that on arrival at Eugene the crew on No. 717 will find that this move will not work. There may be other traffic in the track behind the pickup, the track may be out of service behind the pickup, or the pickup may be in a track that only opens at the west end. There is an alternative. No. 717 can put the engine back against the train and wait for Adams to finish at 1540, then pull up to the west crossovers at Eugene on Main 1 and work from the west end. This arrangement still allows No. 717 to arrive at Galveston ahead of the schedule arrival time and does not delay No. 730. Given the readily available alternative, planning on an unusual movement for No. 717's pickup at Eugene is not unreasonable.

Westward / Eastward train planning sheet.

717	715	99	101	5	Train	2 (cf 07)	68 (cf 1050)	102	712	730 (67's par by 1900)
1335	1150	OT1455 / 1315	0950	20ml / 1212	Albany	1148 7ma	1045	OT1645 / 1500	OT1215 / 1455	OT1700 / 1720
					Boston					
1420	1230	1345 / 1415 / 712/102	1020	1232	Chicago / 1230	1128	1008	1415	1410	1635
					Wilson Detroit 24 m1					
1505 / 1600 ol / 1550 pa	1315 / 1400 ol / 1350 pa / 102/712	1445	1050	1252 20ml	Eugene / Adams 1340 24 m1	1108	0933	1340 / (715)	1330(715) / 1310 so	1555 / 1525 pa
				1312 / 13ml	Fargo					
1630	1430	1515			Galveston	1048	0900	1370	1230	1445
OT700	OT400	OT1640 / cf1120						OT1500		

open 1645 · 730 out 1 ct

Fig. 15-46 The diagram below represents the same information found on the trainsheet example on the previous page (Fig. 15-45).

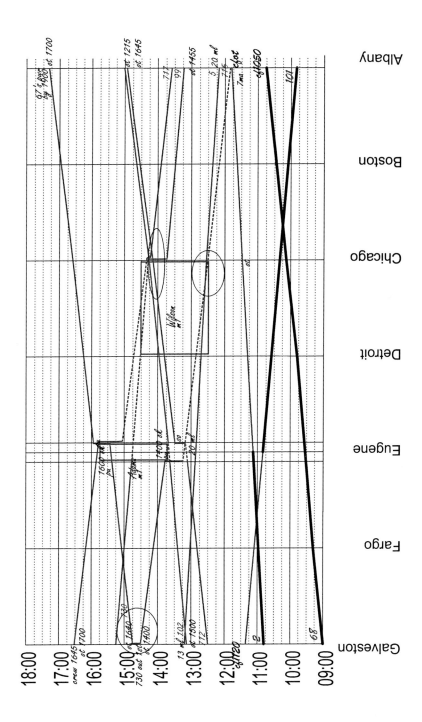

"STRICT PRIORITY" OPERATION

Fig. 15-47 The conflicts are the same as those identified in Fig. 15-37 (page 134). No. 99 and No. 102 must not be delayed for No. 715, No. 717, No. 712, or No. 730, nor may they be delayed for maintenance of way work.

Both tracks are needed between Chicago and Detroit for No. 99 and No. 102 to meet. Wilson will not be able to work on Main 1 until at least 1345. No. 715 can be reversed from Albany to Eugene to allow No. 5 to pass without delay to either train.

No. 715 can use either track at Eugene. The crossovers at East Eugene and West Eugene are arranged to allow either No. 99 or No. 102 to cross over without losing running time. Put No. 715 back on Main 1 at East Eugene. The other traffic will use Main 2. Which track No. 715 uses at Eugene makes no difference in the ability to allow Adams to work on Main 1. If No. 715 is on Main 1, Adams cannot work until 1420, when No. 715 leaves following No. 99. If No. 715 is on Main 2, Adams cannot work until 1415, when No. 99 passes.

Tell Adams that he cannot have Main 1 at Eugene until 1415 or 1420. He says that his supervisor does not want the work done on overtime, so he will find some other work for the rest of the day.

Westward					Train	Eastward				
717	715	99	101	5		2 (of 07)	68 (of 1050)	102	712	730 (67's pwr by 1900)
1335	1150	OT 1455 / 1315	0950	20ml / 1212	Albany	1148 7ma	1045	OT1645 / 1440	OT1215 / 1455	OT1700 / 1720
	(5)			(715)	Boston					1635
1415	1230	1345	1020	1232	Chicago	1128	1008	1410 (712)	1410 (102)	
					Wilson Detroit 24mt / 1230					
1500 1600 ok / 1530 pa	1315 1400 ok / 1420 pa	1415	1050	1252 / 20ml	Eugene Adams 1330 24mt	1108	0933	1340	1330	1555 / 1525 pa
	(99)				Fargo				1310 so	
1610 OT7700	1500 OT7400	1445 OT7640	of 1120	1312 / 13ml	Galveston	1048	0900	1310 OT1500	1230	1445

crew 1645 oat 1st

Fig. 15-48 The diagram below represents the same information found on the trainsheet example on the previous page (Fig. 15-47).

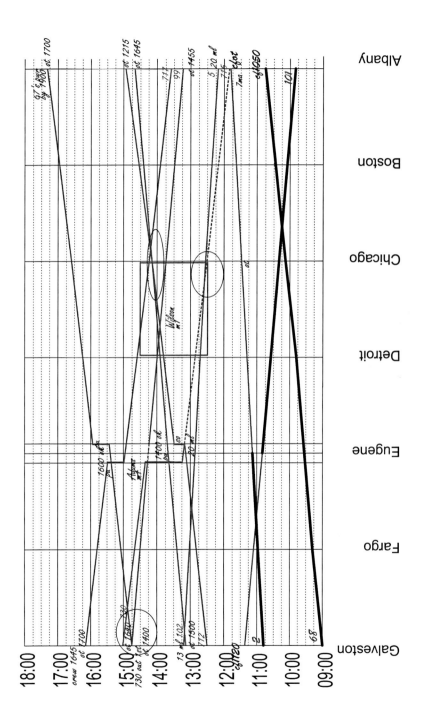

Fig. 15-49 No. 712 cannot leave Eugene ahead of No. 102 and cannot work at Eugene ahead of No. 102 because of No. 715 working on Main 1. No. 102 cannot pass No. 712 between Galveston and Eugene without delay because of No. 5. The train handling instructions say that in this situation, No. 712 should be held at Galveston for No. 102 to avoid delay to No. 102. However No. 712 is a through train and the yard says there is no room to hold it for No. 102. The other side says that right now they are over an hour apart and holding No. 712 somewhere for No. 102 to overtake is not possible.

Let No. 712 run regular (Main 2) from Galveston to West Eugene and hold it there for No, 102 to pass. After No. 5 arrives at Galveston, reverse (Main 1) No. 102 from Galveston to West Eugene to pass No. 712. No. 102 goes back to Main 2 at West Eugene and No. 712 will follow.

No. 712 has time on arrival at West Eugene to make a cut on the setout, pull it through the yard, and return on Main 2 before No. 102 arrives. No. 712 will be ready to follow No. 102 when it passes.

No. 99 will reverse from East Eugene to West Eugene to pass No. 715. No. 715 will be ready to follow No. 99 when it passes.

Westward | cf 07 | cf 1050 | Eastward | 67's pwr by 1900

717	715	99	101	5	Train	2	68	102	712	730
		OT 1455		20ml	Albany	1148		OT1645	OT1215	OT1700
1335	1150	1315	0950	1212		7ma	1045	1445	1515	1720
					Boston					
	(5)			(715)						
	1230		1020		Chicago	1128	1008	1415	1430	1635
1415		1345		1232						
					Wilson 1230 Detroit					
					2h m1				(102)	
1500 1600 ok	1315 1400 ok		1050	1252	Eugene	1108	0933	1345	1350	1555
1530 pu	1420 pu	1415		20ml	~~Adams 1330 2h m1~~				1310 so	1525 pu
	(99)				Fargo					
								(5)		
1610	1500	1445		1312	Galveston	1048	0900	1315	1230	1445
OT1700	OT1400			13ml				1310		

crew 1645 | 730 out 1st | OT1640 | cf 1120 | OT1500

Fig. 15-50 The diagram below represents the same information found on the trainsheet example on the previous page (Fig. 15-49).

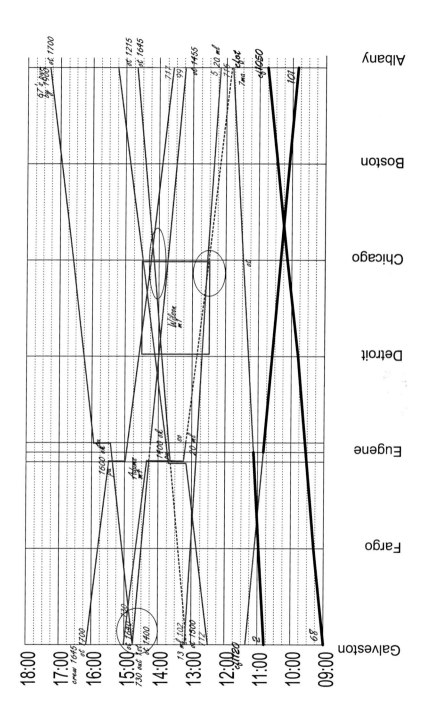

Fig. 15-51 The last remaining conflict is between No. 717 and Wilson on Main 1 between Chicago and Eugene. If Wilson goes to work right behind No. 99 (1345 at Chicago), he can be finished at 1545. No. 717 is not an important train, so it would be acceptable to allow Wilson to work by holding No. 717. Ask Wilson if he can use the two hours on Main 1 after 1345. He says that he can do that and still finish his workday on time, so No. 717 will wait at Chicago, but not until Wilson is finished.

After No. 102 and No. 712 are by Chicago, No. 717 can use Main 2 from Chicago to East Eugene, crossing over to Main 1 before No. 730 arrives.

	Westward					Train			Eastward			
	of 1120					of 07	of 1050				67's pwr by 1900	
717	715	99	101	5			2	68	102	712	730	
		OT1455				Albany	1148 7ma		OT1645	OT1215	OT1700	
1335	1150	1315	0950	20ml 1212				1045	1445	1515	1720	
	(5)			(715)		Boston						
1415	1230	1345	1020	1232		Chicago	1128	1008	1415	1430	1635	
1430												
(712)						Wilson Detroit 1345 2h m						
1515 1000 ob	1375 1400 ob	1415	1050	1252 20ml		Eugene Adams 1330 2h mt	1108	0933	1345	1350	1555	
1545 pa	1420 pa									(102)		
				1312 13ml		Fargo				1310 so	1525 pa	
1625	1500	1445				Galveston	1048	0900	1375	1230	1445	
OT1700	OT1400	OT1640							1310			

open 1645   730 out 1st   OT1500

Fig. 15-52 The diagram below represents the same information found on the trainsheet example on the previous page (Fig. 15-51).

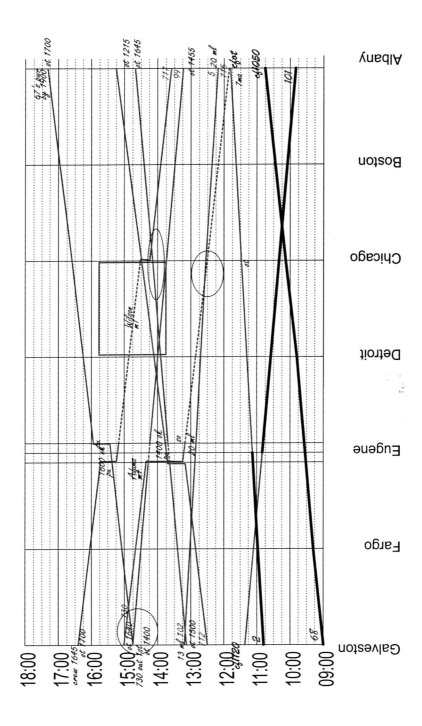

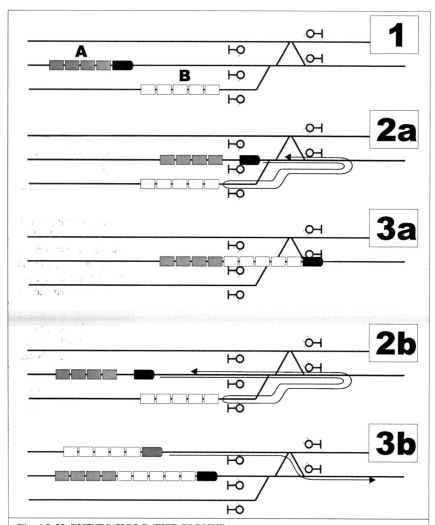

Fig. 15-53 **CUT TO HOLD THE PICKUP**

1. An arriving train (A) will pick up a cut of cars (B). 2a. The crew will normally stop at the switch leading to the pickup, or at the signal if it is an interlocking or CTC control point. After cutting off the engine, they will pull over the switch, back against the cars and double to the train. 3a. After doubling, the train will block the switch or interlocking/control point until it leaves. 2b. If another movement must be made through the switch or the interlocking/control point before the train picking up leaves, the crew can be instructed (in advance) to cut to hold the pickup. The crew will stop far enough from the switch or signal to accommodate the cars to be picked up and the engine. 3b. After doubling together, the train picking up will be clear of the switch or interlocking/control point.

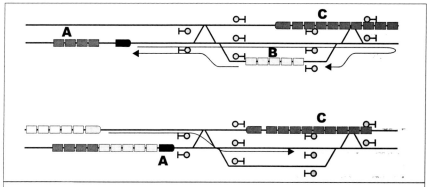

15-54 Working at the wrong end of the yard.

Pickups are generally made by stopping the head end of the train as close as possible to the head end of the pickup (Fig. 15-53). Doubling to the train involves a relatively short movement. Setouts are generally made in the same manner. A traffic situation may make working from the "wrong end" of the yard preferable. Such situations are found in the discussion of Fig. 15-13, 15-45, and 15-49. In Fig.15-13 the siding is not available for No. 712 because of track maintenance. In the others, there is time for a crew to make the pickup or setout, but not time to leave ahead of another train.

(Top) Trains A and C are arriving, each with work in the yard. After picking up, train A must be passed by another train before leaving. Train A cuts at the near end of the yard to hold the pickup, runs to the far end with the engine and gets against the pickup. When ready to move, the engine shoves the pickup against the train.

(Bottom) Train A is together and ready to go. Train C is stopped, cut off, and ready to work in the yard when the traffic clears. One main track remains clear for the train overtaking Train A.

Making a long shove is not convenient. The time consumed by the pickup will be longer than by a pickup performed in the normal way, but when the traffic situation makes this type of movement desirable, the extra time doubling together is offset by the reduced time between arriving and leaving (waiting for other traffic before picking up or setting out in a more convenient manner).

Weather and the length of the pickup must be considered when planning a traffic arrangement that involves this type of movement. One crewmember must ride on the leading end of the movement when shoving from the yard to the train. The shove may be several thousand feet (the length of the pickup plus the amount of clear yard track behind the pickup plus the length of the interlocking limits between the train and the pickup). Severe weather adds to the difficulty of this type of movement. Making a setout in this manner is not as difficult under extreme conditions as making a pickup because the forward movement pulls the cars into the yard track and the reverse movement is made with only the engine.

The train crew must be notified in advance if a pickup or setout is to be made in this manner.

HOW FAR SHOULD THE DISPATCHER FIGURE?

Every train dispatcher, chief dispatcher, yardmaster, and terminal manager should come on duty to a plan that lasts a minimum of half of a shift. That gives time to look into the supporting activities and plan beyond the end of the current plan. To that end, a train dispatcher should publish at least 12 hours of traffic if possible. The trains on the road and expected within at least half of the next dispatcher shift should be figured in the manner described. Trains beyond that time can be figured using some normal running times and an estimated figure for each opposing train that may be met (on a single track line) or following train that may pass.

The longest meet delay for a train that must not be delayed will generally be twice the longest running time between sidings (Fig. 13-1 page 24). Most meet delays for these trains will be much less. A reasonable long-range estimate is the average running time between sidings.

The longest meet delay for any other train will generally be half of the longest running time between sidings. A reasonable long-range estimate is one-fourth of the average running time between sidings for each of these trains that will be met.

The longest delay to be overtaken by another train will generally be the greatest difference in running time between stations at which the train may be overtaken. On a multiple track line, those stations may be sidings or if the line has bi-directional signaling, controlled crossovers. For each train that will overtake, a reasonable long-range delay estimate is half of the average difference (between the train being figured and the faster train) in running time between stations at which the train may be overtaken.

Adjust these figures for traffic situations that will apparently affect the train being figured. For example, if closely spaced trains will be overtaken or will meet an opposing train, delays to the second will generally be greater than delays to the first unless the passing or meeting point will accommodate both trains. A reasonable long-range estimate is that the headway between trains that must meet opposing traffic on a single track line will be twice the average running time between sidings. For trains that will be overtaken on a double track current of traffic line with sidings, a reasonable long-range estimate is that the headway between trains that will be overtaken will be the difference in running time between sidings for the faster and slower trains. Double track with bi-directional traffic, controlled crossovers, and no sidings will have a different effect on closely following trains that will be overtaken. If there is opposing traffic, the use of both tracks in the same direction for overtaking will generally be limited. Generally the first of two trains being overtaken will be delayed and the second will close up on the first. A reasonable long-range estimate for trains that will be overtaken under these conditions is that after being overtaken, the first train will subsequently be running on the expected times of the second and the second will be on the block of the first.

PUBLISH THE PLAN

The game of train operation is played on many boards simultaneously. The game is not over when the person handling any one of the boards gets the pieces to the goal, because that is just the starting point on the next person's board. The best plan is of little good if the dispatcher on the territory is the only one to know about it. There is little benefit in working out an elaborate plan to keep all of the trains moving just to have them come to a stop at the starting line of the next person's game board.

TERMINALS AND ADJACENT DISPATCHERS

Dispatchers are generally required to periodically publish some type of lineup to terminals and adjoining dispatcher districts. In addition, the dispatcher will receive many requests for fresh figures. Finally, the dispatcher will probably publish a call figure on each train. All of these figures should be as accurate as possible. Most of the figures will be used to build a plan that affects the figures the recipient has published to the dispatcher. If you miss a figure by two hours, it will probably affect one or more of the times the recipient has published to you. If none of the figures are worth the paper they are written on, the figures received will probably also not be worth the paper they are written on. This problem can be self-sustaining with a constant stream of bad information feeding a constant stream of bad information.

If some event such as a grade crossing collision or a broken rail substantially delays a train, the dispatcher should make every effort to quickly publish the information to at least the adjoining dispatcher or terminal. This information could materially affect the plan on the adjoining game board.

MAINTENANCE OF WAY

The dispatcher can sometimes improve track maintenance productivity similarly. Much of the maintenance work requires some advance preparation time for clearing the line and relinquishing the authority. Some maintenance workers may ask if there is more before beginning to clear so that if there is, they will not waste the time of putting away equipment, making the track safe, and traveling to a place where they can clear. Others may not. In some situations it may be helpful to broadcast on the radio the delay of a train that may result in significant extra working time.

This is just an example. It is not necessarily appropriate for all situations, but the concept of keeping the maintenance work in mind when things change is. Dispatchers will also find that if the maintenance workers become accustomed to this consideration, they will be less likely to overstay permits. Dispatchers will find also that they are quite likely to get track back from maintenance work if it is physically possible after broadcasting something like:

> *Dispatcher to Jones, Smith, and Brown between Eugene and Galveston, my figure on 51 was no good and he's 30 minutes faster than what I gave you.*

When appropriate, the reverse can also be used:

> *Dispatcher to Jones, Smith, and Brown between Eugene and Galveston, my figure on 51 was no good and he's 30 minutes later than what I gave you. If you need more call and I'll pass it out to you.*

TRAINS

Publishing the plan can also include giving information to trains that are on the road. Trains are very heavy vehicles that require rather a great amount of energy to accelerate and decelerate. Stopping a 60 mph train then accelerating again to 60 mph requires much more energy, thus much more fuel, than slowing the 60 mph train to 50 mph and accelerating to 60 mph. Less time is also lost when a train reduces speed instead of stopping. When practical and appropriate, if a train will be delayed for only a few minutes for the arrival of an opposing train, advance information to the engineer of the train that will be delayed will allow adjusting the speed. Tell the engineer what time the opposing train is expected to be in the clear. The engineer can adjust the speed as needed to minimize the reduction in speed or avoid stopping.

Also consider notifying in advance trains that will receive extended delays. If a long delay will occur at an isolated location, notify the crew in advance of the last place where it would be possible to walk a short distance to a store or restaurant. Even if they don't have sufficient time to have a meal in a restaurant, the opportunity to obtain food or beverages to go will be welcome. Tell them what time they must arrive at the waiting point or what time they must leave the place they will stop. If they leave the train, make sure they bring a radio and can hear you in case the situation changes. If they cannot bring a radio or radio reception is not good at that location, one crewmember must remain on the engine to listen to the radio and use the locomotive horn to summon the rest of the crew if necessary. If the extended delay will occur at a location where a store or restaurant is within walking distance from the train, use the same procedure after the train has stopped where the delay will occur.

STRATEGY AND TACTICS

Two definitions are important to the train dispatcher.

Strategy: The carefully laid plan made before engaging the opponent.

Tactics: The plan made necessary by the opponent after the engagement has begun.

For the train dispatcher, the opponent is the unpredictable "things" that happen (e.g. locomotives fail, signals fail, rails break).

Train dispatchers must be aware of the almost complete impossibility of carrying all elements of a long-range plan through to conclusion. Were it that easy, there would be no need for train dispatchers.

One might question the need for the strategic planning that has been described if elements will change as time passes. A new tactic can be much more quickly developed from a strategic plan than from repeatedly re-calculating all of the trains and maintenance activity. The railroad will operate much more efficiently from a plan than it will from constant reaction to problems. Ultimately, working from a plan instead of reacting requires less time and effort from the train dispatcher. The dispatcher is also less likely to stop trains while figuring out what to do with them. Stopping trains while figuring aggravates the situation that is causing the change in plan.

In the single track planning example, No. 5 leaves Albany at 1222 instead of the 1212 that was projected. No. 5 affects two trains directly. No. 715 is already in the siding at Boston. There is not enough time to move No. 715. No. 712 still cannot make Eugene for No. 5. No immediate action is required. Are there collateral effects? No. 715 has been delayed by ten minutes, but must wait at Eugene for No. 712 to finish working and leave. No. 712 will arrive at Eugene ten minutes later, but will no longer need to wait for Adams to clear the siding. That reduces No. 712's time at Eugene to twenty minutes instead of thirty. No. 712 will leave Eugene at 1355 as planned (in spite of the ten minute delay) and nothing else changes. The effect of the delay to No. 5 at Albany is apparent in seconds. No new figuring is necessary.

The opponent is not always so kind. At 1245 (in the single track example), Adams calls. He would have finished his planned work on time, but he has discovered a broken rail in the siding. He has called Wilson to come with his crew and fix the rail. He says that Wilson should have the track ok for service at 1415. The direct effect is immediately apparent. No. 712 can set out but the engine cannot return to the train until 1415. The plan has No. 715 holding the main track while No. 712 works. The west end of the yard is available, so No. 715 can make the pickup if it is not blocked by No. 712's train. No. 715 must meet No. 730 at Fargo and cannot leave there until 1505, so there is no hurry to move No. 715 after doing the work. If No. 715 is instructed to clear between switches at Eugene after picking up, No. 712 can leave Fargo at 1415. No. 715 can leave Eugene at 1435 on No. 712's arrival and still reach Fargo before No. 712.

Wilson calls to release the siding at 1420. When asked about the work between Detroit and Chicago, he responds that there is not enough time to drive to the work location, set up, and finish before the shift ends, so he is done for the day.

The only reason for the meet between No. 712 and No. 717 at Chicago was to allow Wilson time to finish the work between Chicago and Detroit. That is no longer necessary. If No. 717 meets No. 712 at Detroit, it will be delayed 35 minutes for No. 712. If No. 717 is not delayed for No. 712, it can arrive at Eugene at 1500; five minutes after No. 712 has finished working. That seems like a good move, but is it?

No. 730 can arrive at Eugene at 1525. No. 717 can finish working by 1530, but must pull west of Eugene to work, preventing No. 730 from leaving Fargo until 1530. No. 717 could then leave Eugene at 1550 on the arrival of No. 730 instead of 1555. The five minutes of time made up serves no purpose because there is no crew at Galveston until 1645, 10 minutes after the originally planned arrival. Meeting No. 712 and No. 717 at Eugene would result in five minutes delay to No. 712 and 25 minutes delay to No. 730 that would accomplish nothing.

If No. 717 meets No. 712 at Detroit, No. 717 will arrive at Eugene ten minutes later, will not affect No. 730, and will arrive at Galveston ten minutes later; the same time the connecting crew is available.

The appropriate tactical move is apparent in seconds when working from a carefully constructed strategic plan. Calculating all of the effects of the broken rail might take several minutes. Merely reacting with what look like "good meets" could result in unnecessary delay.

16. THE MECHANICS OF HANDLING TRAINS

This is the visible part of train dispatching. It is often mistakenly considered train dispatching. Issuing orders, whether electronically, in writing, or verbally is just one of the steps. It looks easy; in fact it looks so easy to someone who doesn't know about the part that can't be seen that it has been a source of trouble for train dispatchers for many years. The goal of technological development has generally been facility in issuing authority. Facility in issuing authority is accompanied by an increase in traffic and/or territory. There are times that a train dispatcher's territory is so busy that authority, whether electronic, written, or verbal cannot be issued fast enough. By the time the situation has reached this point, critical has come and gone. If the dispatcher can't push buttons, write, or talk fast enough, there is no thinking, no planning, and no attention to detail.

ELECTRONIC CONTROL

Electronic control generally means CTC. CTC may be entirely manually operated, semi-automatic, computer-assisted, or computer-controlled. Older CTC control machines have a hard-wired model board with lights, relay logic and relay code transmission. Newer equipment is microprocessor based with CRT displays, and electronic logic and electronic code transmission.

Understanding what is seen on the model board or CRT display is of primary importance. What is visible on the model board or display is *not* what is occurring in the field. One should never assume that it is. The display is a model representing what is going on in the field. It is updated on a very frequent basis, sufficiently so that it usually appears to be simultaneous with activity in the field. Microprocessor systems process the information faster than relay systems, but the information in the display may still not be exactly what is taking place in the field. If the display shows the condition in the field correctly, it is in correspondence. If it does not, it is out of correspondence.

Two types of electronic messages, control and indication, are the basis of Centralized Traffic Control. Control messages are sent from the office to the field to control signal equipment. Indication messages are sent from the field to the office to update the office display. Generally, processing and communication of control information takes precedence over indication information. If the dispatcher lines a number of switches and/or signals in rapid succession, indication information will wait until all of the control information has been sent. During this time, if changes occur in the field, they will not be represented on the display. Communication failure may also affect correspondence. A communication failure immediately after a control has been sent will result in a change in the field that is not represented on the display.

Generally, the display will give important information about the correspondence of the model. If a signal appliance such as a switch or signal is represented by a continuous, or solid, indication, it is in correspondence with the field. If it is represented by a flashing indication, it is not. When a signal is called, the indication in the office begins flashing. The situation is signal lined in the office, at stop in the field. When the signal in the field clears, the display shows signal lined in the office and lined in the field. If the signal is taken down, the office indication begins flashing. The situation is signal at stop in the office not at stop in the field. When the signal in the field returns to stop, the signal indication in the office is in correspondence. Switches work similarly. If a switch is reversed, the office indication is reverse, the field is not reverse, and the indication flashes. When the switch is reverse in the field, the indication is solid. Switches have a third condition. The detection system looks at normal and reverse, but there is a time when the points are transiting between the two during which neither condition applies. A switch indication is flashing reverse, for example, does not mean reverse in the office and normal in the field. It means reverse in the office and *not reverse* in the field.

Dispatchers should make no assumptions about the state of signal equipment. Interpret the information literally. If a signal was taken down to allow maintenance authority and the indication continues flashing, assume the signal in the field is still lined. The signal may be out of correspondence because the control setting it to stop was never received in the field. If a switch indication is flashing, assume that it is lined for neither route.

MANUALLY OPERATED

Manually operated CTC is the most labor intensive for train dispatchers, but gives the greatest degree of control. Train performance is affected when a dispatcher "gets behind" the work. Trains begin slowing for yellow signals and stopping for red signals neither of which is associated with traffic. When that happens, the running time changes, which affects the rest of the plan, which causes the dispatcher to become further behind.

The way to keep from getting behind is to plan and work to the plan. CTC is deceptively simple. It is possible to move trains and generally keep them going without thinking about it. A common approach is to line the signal or signals at a station if the train can make it to the station beyond without encountering another train. If another train will be encountered, handle it by putting one in the siding, crossing one over, or some other arrangement that will resolve the conflict. Reality strikes when that method results in a big delay to important trains or in 4 trains at the same 1-train siding at one time.

Don't play video game trains with CTC. Work from a plan. A train dispatcher should not need to figure out at each station whether to line a signal for an approaching train. That's a sure way of getting behind.

During the regular working hours of track maintenance forces, they may unexpectedly appear anywhere at any time. That doesn't mean that signals should not be lined in advance of trains. The running time in a section between controlled signals, and often in two sections, is generally less than the minimum productive time that can be authorized for track maintenance. There is much less chance of delaying a train with 20 or 30 minutes of green in front of it than a train with 10 or 15 minutes. Outside of normal track maintenance time, line each train at least that far in advance. If traffic is heavy and attention should be concentrated on other trains, line signals in advance to the next place the plan calls for the train to be stopped. (This method is not the same as instructions that might be issued requiring two, four, or more signals lined in front of a "hot" train at all times.)

The plan is most likely to change while trains are stopped. Station work may take longer than anticipated. A stop to check a problem with a train may result in an extended delay. Except for passenger train stops that are reliably consistent, require trains to report ready to leave and don't line a signal to leave the station until the train is ready to go. When the train reports, check against the anticipated leaving time to determine if the train must be re-figured. If a train reports that it has stopped because of a problem, take down signals that are lined for it and instruct the train to advise when moving again. Taking a signal back from a train is a more time consuming process (because of the need to contact the engineer of the train, explain the situation and receive an acknowledgment) than lining it when the train is ready to move.

Under some conditions, lining the leaving signal at a station where a train is stopping for work can be advantageous. For maximum safety, signal spacing and speed is calculated using the greatest anticipated stopping distance under the worst possible conditions. The approach signal may slow a relatively short braking distance train such as a light intermodal train much sooner than necessary. If the train is time-sensitive, an approach indication arriving at the station may cause noticeable delay. The effect is most profound when the leaving signal is the beginning of CTC and the approaching train is in yard limits because the train must reduce to restricted speed rather than the speed prescribed for an approach signal indication. If traffic allows, before the train arrives, instruct the engineer to notify when the train has stopped, then line the signal to leave. When the train has stopped, respond that you will take down the leaving signal and instruct the engineer to call when the train is ready to leave.

The CTC indications can give important information beside the current location of the trains. Sometimes indications from the field can get behind, but often they are sufficiently timely for the figuring a dispatcher must do. Speed and terrain are important to running time. The CTC indications can't give any information about terrain. They can give some information about speed.

Time a train over an OS indication. The length used in calculating is the train in feet plus the length of the control point in feet. An estimate works. The time information is not sufficiently accurate to require precise measurement. The speed in miles per hour is roughly

((train feet+control point feet)/seconds)/1.5.

The speed can be timed again if there is no following train. Line a signal behind the train and count the seconds after the OS circuit clears until the signal clears. The speed in miles per hour is roughly

((feet between signals-control point feet)/seconds)/1.5

Often there are two Block Indicator, or BK, indications between control points. Sometimes the indicators have an overlap in the track they represent, but generally not. Dispatchers should find out where these BK limits are as part of learning the territory. Time can be measured between a control point and the BK split. Time can also be measured as the train crosses the split; from the time the second indication shows until the time the first one is dark. If there is an overlap, the time can be measured for the length of the overlap in the same way that it is measured on an OS circuit.

SEMI-AUTOMATIC

Semi-automatic CTC has several variations that may include:

- Fleeting: once lined, a controlled signal acts like an automatic block signal, clearing again each time the block it governs is clear. This feature may be turned on and off for each signal. Some systems allow the choice of how many times the signal will re-clear after a train before it restores to stop and acts like a controlled signal. This is a very useful tool, but should be used carefully. If used without caution, losing track of trains and perhaps getting a train in an undesired position can result.

- Stacking: Some CTC control machines allow future movements to be lined in advance. Trains may be lined east on the main track at the west end and west into the siding at the east end. Then the train in the siding may be lined out the west end and the train on the main may be lined to leave on the main at the east end. After the first movement at each end of the siding clears, the switch and signal are automatically lined for the next movement.

- Automatic: On some control machines, individual locations may be set to automatic operation. When a train hits the approach to the control point at the initial station of a siding, the machine checks to see if a train is lined through the next control location in the opposite direction. If the next control location is not lined in the opposite direction, the machine lines the approaching train down the main at both ends of the siding. If the leaving signal is lined against the approaching train at the next station, the approaching train is lined into the siding.

Each of these, used correctly, is a very powerful tool. Each, used incorrectly, merely automates poor train dispatching practices.

The most effective use of any of these tools is in conjunction with a comprehensive plan for train movement. One of the oldest principles of train dispatching is that if everything is operating as planned, the train dispatcher has little to do. When something is not operating according to plan, the dispatcher's effort should be directed to the problem. Automation can be used to keep the parts of the territory that are operating as planned moving with minimal attention while greater attention is given to parts of the line with problems.

Care must be taken that trains needing specific tracks for station work, wide load clearance, or other reasons are not routed incorrectly when using automatic features. If trains are longer than some sidings, the dispatcher must ensure that automation does not make a meet in a place where neither train fits. During hours when maintenance of way forces are working, dispatchers should be cautious when protecting work that automatic features have not called for a signal in the field that has not yet indicated in the office. Some systems may allow track blocking to be put in place when a signal called by an automatic feature is pending.

Most important in the use of automation is to know what is going on. The dispatcher should monitor trains being handled by automation as closely as if the signals were lined individually. If something has changed, take down the automation ahead of the affected trains. If a train must be on a certain track somewhere, don't set automation to handle signals and switches at that station.

Automatic functions do not use sophisticated methods to determine that a train has passed and the next instruction in the list is the current one. A momentary signal failure can cause the controlled signal to display stop and the system to consider that the instruction that called the signal has been fulfilled. The failure clears and the next instruction calls the signal, and perhaps switches for another route. Perhaps the fourth train must use the main track at a station because it has a wide load that cannot use the siding. The fifth train must use the siding because of a setout on a track connected to the siding. The instructions are stacked and the dispatcher goes on about other work. After the third train, the system calls for the main track route and a signal for the fourth train. There is a momentary failure that drops the OS circuit then clears itself, unobserved by the dispatcher. The system considers the failure to be the passage of the fourth train and executes the next instruction, which lines the fourth train into the siding.

A similar situation can occur in heavy traffic territory with many short movements. A local calls to leave Boston for Detroit. There is a fleet of westward trains, three of which have passed. The dispatcher tells the local that it is close, but if they can go right now they can run to Detroit ahead of the approaching high priority train. The local says that they are ready to go now and the dispatcher **LINES THEM UP** (lines the switches for the route and clears the signals). One of two things can occur (mostly because an important train is involved and that is when these things happen):

*   The signals at Chicago and Detroit are set for fleet and the local stops on the main track at Detroit (with the high priority train right behind) because the wrong route is lined,

- The dispatcher cancels the fleet function at Detroit and stacks three movements down the main, one for the yard, and one down the main. Several minutes later, with the important train approaching, the local calls to say that they had some trouble with the pickup and aren't ready to go. There is just enough time to take back the signal, wait for the time release, and line the main track route without delay to the important train. Twenty minutes later, the important train is stopped at the signal at Detroit, asking why they are lined into the yard.

Don't let automation set up something you did not intend to have occur.

COMPUTER ASSISTED

Computer assisted dispatching uses software to make train dispatching decisions. The sophistication of the software may vary from installation to installation. The software may require the train dispatcher to input data to support the decisions the software makes. The train dispatcher may need to monitor the decisions made by the computer and override the decisions that do not produce the desired result. The dispatcher generally remains responsible for publishing information about train movements, setting crew calls, etc. Publishing accurate figures may be made difficult by the decision making process of the software. If the software is too sensitive to system change, it may change plans so frequently that it is impossible to predict what will happen. Computer assisted systems also eliminate most of the dispatcher-train interface. If the dispatcher must periodically do something for each train, such as line signals, it is much easier to remember what trains are on the road and where they are. Dispatchers must be much more diligent with computer assisted systems. All of the traffic should be reviewed repeatedly, just as it is in non-automated systems. If the dispatcher does not constantly review the traffic, an undesirable situation set up by the software may be executed. If the dispatcher does not have a thorough knowledge of the traffic on the line, valuable time may be wasted in an emergency situation.

FAILURE

The failure of an electronic control system requires an extreme degree of caution. The electronic control system is the means of issuing instructions to trains. This aspect of electronic control is of the least concern if there is a failure of the system. The electronic control system provides train location information and the means of protecting movements. These two elements are of great concern.

The Nature of the Failure

A control system failure may not become evident for some time. A control system failure usually involves communication failure between the field and the office. The failure might be in the communication equipment in the field, the communication equipment in the office, or the link connecting the two. The field equipment at each control point will continue to operate as a local interlocking. Some systems have a local interlocking control panel in the bungalow at each control point to allow normal operation in the case of a control system failure. Each bungalow becomes an interlocking tower for the duration of the control system failure as long as it is attended by a control operator (usually a signal department employee). If there is no local control panel or if a bungalow has a local control panel but is not attended, the interlocking functions like any other unattended interlocking. A control system failure might involve office control equipment and result in the complete loss of the train and track display information.

Generally, the indication of a control system failure is a train that does not appear to be where it should or a control sent for a switch or signal receives no indication (continues to show out of correspondence). Because the display is based on intermittent information, it will represent the situation as of the last information received before the failure, not the situation when the failure occurred.

A westward train clears the control point at the west switch of Boston at 0910. It shows in the approach to the west switch at Boston and will continue to do so until it reaches the beginning of the east approach circuit of the east switch at Chicago at 0920. At 0920 the system fails an instant before the train reaches the east approach circuit to the east switch at Chicago. The correct interpretation of the display is that the train has left the east switch at Boston, not that it has not yet reached the east approach circuit to the east switch at Chicago.

Train dispatchers should always recognize the difference between the situation displayed by the control system and the conditions in the field. If there is any evidence of failure, however, all displayed information is suspect until the system is found to be working correctly at the location of the displayed information. A failure may be confined to a single bungalow, to a series of bungalows that have a common communication link, or it may affect an entire district.

Unless the failure is an office control equipment failure, the first step is to determine the magnitude of the problem. This should be done in preference to any other activity. Start at the control point at which the failure was first noticed. Work in one direction, moving away from that control point, determining whether other control points appear to be active. Some control machines have a recall function and an indication of control and indication activity. This function is the preferred means of checking because it makes no changes to switches or signals. If it is not available, operate a switch at each control point if possible. A signal should not be used to test control point response unless there is no other signal appliance that can be used (switch, derail, snow melter, or other equipment that provides an indication in response to a condition). Using a signal to test control system response may result in unintentional authority for train movement. Remember when testing that only the control or the indication functions may be affected. It is possible to drop a signal in the face of a train that appears somewhere else on the display. It is also possible that a switch doesn't appear to respond because of a control failure and that a change in condition such as the approach of a train will be indicated properly. After finding the end of the failure or reaching the end of the district in the first direction, start at the control point at which the failure was first noticed and work the other way. The result of this testing will provide enough information for a call to the signal maintainer or technician as well as the basis of the information needed to continue operating trains.

Train Location Information

Accurate and current train location information is essential to the efficient control of train movement and maintenance of way activity. When the control system is operating normally, train movements are authorized by signal indication and the office and field control system equipment provide protection. Maintenance of way authority is issued based upon the information on the control system track display. If the control system fails, movements are generally authorized by verbal or written authority, accurate train location information is essential to safety. The train location record is the key element in preventing conflicting movements when the signal system is not providing protection.

Once the extent of the failure has been determined and the appropriate assistance has been called, the next step is determining the location of all trains and all maintenance of way forces authorized to occupy the track in the affected area. Older control machines with a permanent display panel allowed pieces of paper representing trains to be taped directly to the display and moved as a new location was reported. This method is not practical with electronic displays. Obtain a sheet of paper large enough (or several sheets of paper and tape) to create a trainsheet, a diagram, or a model board (track diagram). If using a model board, markers representing trains will also be needed. The markers should be of sufficient size and weight to maintain position. An eraser is well suited to the purpose. A straight pin or a bent paper clip can hold a paper tag with the train identification. This method is the same as that used in early air traffic control. The shortcoming of using a model board instead of a trainsheet or diagram is the same as that of the control system display; it displays the current location of trains but does not provide a means of projection and planning.

The time and train location should be recorded first when a train calls for instructions at a stop signal. Any other train location information (such as failed equipment detector reports or radio conversations that provide train location information) should be recorded for use in planning. Secondary information (not reported by the train or by a person at a known location who is qualified on the operating rules, has identified the train and observed that it is complete) should not be used as evidence of train location when issuing potentially conflicting movement authority to another train.

Protecting Movements

Unless the control points are being operated from the local control panels, protection of train movements during a control system failure requires the same procedure whether the failure coves the entire district or only a single control point. Each train should be authorized to pass each stop signal it encounters after it arrives at the signal. The arriving time at that location should be noted on the record of train movement being used during the failure. Before authorizing the train to pass the stop signal, check the record of train movement for opposing traffic on that track.

Talking trains by red signals and using signals to protect maintenance of way work are not compatible practices. CTC permits, Track and Time, and similar authority should not be given in an area of control system failure. Often, an extensive control system failure is a result of a severe weather event that requires extensive maintenance of way work (e.g. a flood or blizzard). The distance involved and the amount of traffic to be handled are the determining factors for a decision on method of operation.

If the distance is relatively short, the line is open, certain maintenance of way activity must occur regardless of the control system failure, and traffic not related to the maintenance of way activity must be handled, handling the traffic with permission to pass stop signals is appropriate. The maintenance of way work cannot be protected by this method of operation. Instead, the essential maintenance of way activity should be protected by the instructions usually used for maintenance of way work under traffic, such as

---

MEN AND EQUIPMENT WORKING ON MAIN TRACK

BETWEEN MP 9 AND MP 12

0900 UNTIL 1500

PROCEED THROUGH LIMITS ONLY AS DIRECTED BY FOREMAN WILSON

Normally, maintenance of way forces are required to request such authority the previous day; however, the control system failure presents a special set of conditions.

- maintenance of way forces could not anticipate the control system failure,
- trains cannot move through the failure area without specific verbal instructions from the train dispatcher.

As long as the train dispatcher carefully follows a procedure to ensure that each train authorized to enter the control system failure area has the instructions applicable to the area, there is no danger.

If the distance is long, the failure is associated with extensive damage to the line, and train traffic is associated with maintenance of way forces restoring the line, a practical method of handling traffic is the use of CTC permits, Track and Time, or similar authority. Such authority must be protected by controlled signals, so the limits of each authority are the first station outside of either end of the control system failure. All authority issued uses the same limits and specifies joint authority with others as appropriate.

Although the line is effectively out of service, it may be necessary for the train dispatcher to maintain control. For example, flood damage may require three work trains to move material to the damaged locations. The control system failure may include many miles of line and include several stations with sidings. After protecting all movements and maintenance of way activity with CTC permits or similar authority, verbal traffic control is reasonable. Instruct maintenance of way forces and work trains to find a way to contact the dispatcher at or after a certain time (often an event that causes extensive damage also has some effect on the communication facilities). Instruct work trains to call before leaving specific limits. For example, after issuing the appropriate authority for a work train between Albany and Eugene, add

> *The Chicago radio is out, so I probably won't be able to hear you west of Boston. The 0600 rock train is around Chicago and should be looking for another run to the pit any time. The 0900 job with the ditcher is somewhere between Boston and Chicago and is supposed to listen for you*

on the radio. Call the 0900 from the west switch at Boston
when you get there, he's got the 6774, and call me when
you've got him.

Operating During a Control System Failure

The nature and extent of the failure are the significant factors involved in the decision of how to continue operation during the failure or to discontinue operation during the failure. The failure might be limited to a single control point. In that case, handling trains is treated no differently than for any other case of signal failure. Each train calls when stopped at that location and is given permission to pass the stop signal if and when appropriate.

Some railroads may prefer to stop operations during a control system failure. Such a policy may be appropriate if there has been an office equipment failure resulting in a complete loss of the control system. It may not always be appropriate or practical, however. For example, a derailment destroys the bungalow at the west switch at Boston. This in turn causes a control system failure affecting both switches at Chicago and both switches at Detroit. The control system may be out of service between the east switch at Boston and the east switch at Eugene for several days. There is generally great effort put into opening the line for traffic after a derailment. Derailed equipment is pushed to the side rather than rerailed immediately and track is given sufficient temporary repair to allow low speed operation. Several additional days waiting for the control system will probably not be acceptable.

The control system failure will probably be apparent at the time of the derailment. Should a derailment cause a control system failure, determine if the control system will be restored when the line is opened. If not, include the appropriate time for control system failure (stop at a signal, call the dispatcher, await a response, issue instructions, hand operate the switches, move at restricted speed to the next controlled signal) when planning.

Some railroads may have an emergency procedure for taking the signal system out of service and operating on written authority. Safely changing operating systems is not a simple undertaking and should be reserved only for extensive system failure that is expected to have a long duration. Trains may be easily notified of the change in operating rules. The instructions are is-sued at the initial station in the same manner as slow orders and maintenance of way under traffic protection. Maintenance of way forces do not report to the train dispatcher for instructions when coming on duty. they may also come on duty at some distant point and drive to a work location in the af-fected territory. The notification procedure must be repeated before the con-trol system is restored. Train and engine crews and maintenance of way forces may not be familiar with all of the rules affecting written authority operation.

NON-ELECTRONIC CONTROL

Non-electronic control includes any of the systems of written instructions authorizing and controlling train movements. There are three varieties of non-electronic control: paper, computer-assisted and verbal.

PAPER

The implementation of paper systems is simple. The train dispatcher has a book of blank forms. The dispatcher writes the instructions on the form as it is being transmitted by radio or telephone to the train crew. In some cases, the dispatcher writes the instructions on the form then sends them by fax to the train crew.

Paper systems place the responsibility for checking traffic and preventing overlapping authority with the train dispatcher. Before issuing authority, the dispatcher must check for opposing trains, trains ahead in dark territory that have been relieved of flagging, work authority and other conditions that should prevent the movement being authorized. When authorizing train movement, communication failure is a serious consideration. The dis-patcher must be certain before authorizing the movement that all track con-dition instructions have been delivered to the train or are included in the movement authority. If the dispatcher authorizes movement, overlooking a track condition instruction, a communication failure would result in the train proceeding without the track condition information.

Accurate train movement records are extremely important when working with paper systems. Train dispatchers are generally required to make accurate and timely records. The importance is greater when handling traffic with paper systems because the records are the only means of checking traffic and ensuring that there is no overlapping authority and that trains all have the required track condition instructions.

No action should be taken for authorization of any train or track maintenance work until the entire movement has been entered on the trainsheet. If the movement will be traveling in both directions, either as a round trip or with work authority, it must be entered fully on both sides of the trainsheet before any action is taken to authorize the movement. All available information about the train or maintenance work, including crew names, on duty times, engines, cars, and work limits should be entered before any work toward authorizing the movement. Each persistent track condition instruction to be delivered to a train must be recorded in the list of instructions for delivery to the train before any action is taken to authorize movement.

All track condition instructions must be listed as required before issuing. Before issuing a track condition instruction, check all movements that have been authorized against the location of the new condition. First priority is trains already authorized through the limits of the condition. The track condition instructions must be issued immediately to trains that have been authorized through the limits of the condition. The longer the delay, the greater the chance that a communication failure will allow the authorized train to proceed through the track condition at normal speed. Second priority is trains that are on the road but have not yet been authorized through the limits of the track condition. Mark the trainsheet clearly for each train that will need the instruction. Do so in a way that will leave no mistake about the need for the track condition before issuing additional authority. Third priority is to issue the instruction in its persistent form to be delivered to trains later as needed. Do not fix any other trains at initial stations until this has been done.

Before authorizing movement, the train dispatcher must check every currently authorized movement for a conflict with the movement to be authorized. Check carefully for

- Trains moving in the opposite direction,

- Trains moving in the same direction that require rear end protection,
- Work authority.

Check every live trainsheet for traffic. There are generally two live trainsheets on the desk for several hours every day from just before midnight until the last train that originated before midnight has completed its trip. Depending upon the length of the district and the type of traffic, there may regularly be two live trainsheets between 2300 and noon. During traffic interruptions such as derailments or severe weather, there may be several live trainsheets.

COMPUTER ASSISTED

Computer assisted written instruction systems eliminate some of the hazard of paper systems. The computer systems perform the conflict check and will not allow the dispatcher to issue overlapping authority. If the dispatcher fails to make the required records of trains with a paper system, there is a chance of overlapping authority. Failure to make the records with a computer assisted system results in the inability to authorize the movement that was not recorded.

Computer assisted written instruction systems also generate some hazard of their own. There is less mental connection with the contents of the track authority when it is prepared on a computer screen than there is when the document is prepared by hand. That means the dispatcher must put conscious effort into review of the location and authority of traffic. There is a danger that the system will incorrectly handle a conflict that the dispatcher has overlooked. The dispatcher reads the intended authority from the copy displayed on the screen, overlooking the line that says

Not in effect until after the arrival of 7653 East

The crewmember repeats the authority exactly as the dispatcher has transmitted it. The dispatcher notices the correct repeat but not the omission from the original displayed on the screen, acknowledging (with the appropriate keystroke) the restriction displayed on the screen without noticing it. This is the reverse of the usual verbal transmission failure, but it has happened.

There is a greater danger that the dispatcher will miss an incorrect repeat when checking by some sort of entry on the keyboard while the train crew repeats. Computer assisted systems may not allow some complex movements or may allow them with only great difficulty. Completely losing track of time while manipulating the computer system, especially when trying to work around its objection to a necessary movement, is extremely easy to do. Losing track of time means losing track of trains. The hazard is great any time a train dispatcher loses track of time and/or the location of trains. If necessary, stop traffic while handling a difficult situation with computer assisted written authority.

VERBAL

Verbal instruction systems have few inherent hazards, because a system of authority and train protection, generally Yard Limits, is in effect concurrently. The system is not foolproof. A train dispatcher can still enter into a hazardous situation in verbal instruction territory. A movement against the current of traffic requires protection, even under yard limit rules. The train dispatcher, before allowing a movement against the current of traffic, must ensure that no trains are operating, or will operate, with the current of traffic. A situation is possible in which a train moving against the current of traffic passes a proceed signal at track speed and encounters a train moving against the current of traffic near the next signal. It is not reasonable to expect a train operating on a proceed indication to be able to stop at the next signal. Track maintenance forces may not be shunting the track, likewise resulting in approaching trains operating on a proceed signal into an occupied track.

Even when the underlying system prevents a collision, failure to consider the traffic and direct appropriately defeats the purpose of assigning a train dispatcher to a terminal territory.

Care should be taken to avoid misunderstanding and ensure compliance when issuing verbal instructions. A small amount of effort expended in ensuring understanding and compliance will result in a much more smoothly operating railroad. A small amount of effort ensuring that the instructions are not forgotten or overlooked will result in safe operation.

If a train or maintenance employee asking for permission to enter the main track must wait for a train to pass, avoid authorizing the movement in advance. After some time has elapsed, the authority may be remembered, but not the wait that precedes it.

If the train should be in sight, ask

> *"Southward train showing there?"*

If the answer is yes, respond with something like

> *That's 2751 south. After he's by 3308 may enter the main track and proceed south.*

If the train is not in sight when it is expected to be or should not be in sight yet, respond

> *Call me back when you see 2751 South pass.*

If the need to wait five minutes for signal protection after opening the switch is a consideration, instruct the crew to call back when the expected train is showing and give authority or permission to move after it passes.

This method helps to ensure that the waiting crew identifies the approaching train and that the waiting crew doesn't, after some period of time, remember the authority and not the restriction. Requiring the waiting crew to call back after the approaching train ensures that the train dispatcher knows what is happening exactly when and allows one more chance to talk to the waiting crew should something change before the approaching train passes.

If authorizing the movement in advance cannot be avoided, be entirely sure that the person receiving the authority understands what will happen. Mention the movement more than once in different ways as a memory aid.

*Since it won't work out for you to call me when 7324 west
shows up, here's a permit. I'll give you an after on him.
Permit Number one to JR Jones on the main track....AF-
TER....7324 west has passed, between Albany and Buffalo
from 0900 until 1100.*

After the repeat:

That is correct. That 7324 west will be up there about 0910.

If the waiting train must see more than one train by, be specific about the
number of trains and the train after which to call. If the order of the trains is
certain, respond with something like

*You're there for three of them. The third one is 2754 South.
Call me when he's by.*

If the order is not certain, respond with something like:

*You're there for three of them. Call me when you have seen
1110 South, 1515 South and 2754 South.*

If associating the train to follow with a figure, be as careful with the figure as
with a figure for the public. If the waiting crew is told

Call after 2745 south. He'll be there in about 25 minutes.

They may not remain in sight of the track before 25 minutes has passed.

Be careful about the wording of instructions when on the radio, a dispatcher's telephone circuit, a code phone, or any other type of circuit that
may allow more than one person to hear the instruction. Two crews may attempt simultaneously to ask permission to cross over to the other main track.
The dispatcher only hears one of them. The response

OK to cross over

may result in the intended train crossing over as well as the train that was not heard. Any time there is a chance that more than one person will hear an instruction, be very clear about the recipient as well as the instruction:

> *2754 south may cross over to the Northward Main at the South end of Albany Yard.*

When an instruction includes only part of a requested movement, add an instruction to call at the completion of the part of the movement that has been authorized.

> *Engine 3456 use the Northward track from AB Junction to the 59 lead switch. Call me at the 59 lead switch.*

Usually in verbal instruction territory, heavy traffic is accompanied with the need to authorize shorter movements than requested. It is easy to lose track of a train under these conditions. The best possible knowledge of the location of all traffic is extremely important. If a train is given authority for part of the requested movement, the crew may not call when they have reached the end of their authority, assuming that the dispatcher sent them there and knows where they are.

If a movement includes activity that will take an unknown amount of time, such as a train doubling out onto the main track and making an air test before leaving, include an instruction to report when the train is actually leaving.

> *Engine 7324 enter the southward track at the middle cross-over and proceed south. Report when you are moving at the middle crossover.*

If there is a possibility that the situation will change and require additional instructions after some time has passed, only authorize the preparatory part of the movement.

> *Engine 7324 enter the southward track at the middle cross-over, make your doubles, test the air, and report ready to leave.*

By issuing the instructions in that way, the dispatcher ensures that the train is not overlooked after it has taken considerable time to get ready.

Never assume a movement is complete because sufficient time for completion has passed. If there is trouble, the crew will attend to the trouble and may forget to tell the dispatcher for some period of time. Always finish an instruction that will take a train clear of the main tracks or off the dispatcher's territory with

> *Report clear of the Northward track.*

or

> *Report when you have passed BC Junction.*

If the movement will foul a main track for a short period, add an instruction to report clear of that track.

> *Engine 7856 cross over from the yard to the southward track at the east end of the Albany Lead. Report clear of the northward track.*

Never use the term "OK" in a response. "OK" in a response may result in many persons asking for some type of authority, who went unheard by the train dispatcher, believing authority was granted. This may occur even if the context of the response was not correct for the request that was not heard. The person making the request expected the request to be granted. The expected term OK may be heard to the exclusion of the rest of the dispatcher's response. Instructions should be precise and as easy to understand as possible.

> *Engine 7220 may enter the main track at the South end of A yard and proceed to the North end of A yard. Call me when you are in the clear.*

KNOW YOUR LIMIT

Regardless of the means of traffic control, the most dangerous thing a dispatcher can do is to attempt the impossible; to push beyond the ability to handle the traffic. The following advice may not be popular with some railroad managers, but it extremely important to self-preservation and safety and should be heeded.

If you feel that you are losing control; if you look at the CTC display and can't associate the various indication lights with real trains and maintenance workers, if you feel yourself taking shortcuts to keep up; if you are scribbling notes about train calls, track conditions, or other important matters; if you catch yourself at the unthinkable, such as starting to send track authority without the required protection; whatever else makes you feel that you are losing control:

STOP!

If there is even a faint possibility that you may have lapped trains, lapped a train with track maintenance, or missed passing out a speed restriction, stop the trains until you are sure.

Don't add to the mess. No new trains, no phone calls, no radio. Until you have a complete handle on what is going on, the possibility of seriously screwing up is great.

If it is safe to do so (you are sure that you have not set up a dangerous condition), get out of the chair and leave your office/cubicle/pod/workstation. Go for coffee, go to the restroom, walk around the hallways or the parking lot. Being agitated and unable to think clearly happened before you realized that you lost control. Being agitated and unable to think clearly must be stopped before you can regain control. If you feel that you may have set up a dangerous situation, it is not safe to leave. Stop all of the traffic. Call trains on the radio and/or set signals at stop (but don't take signals down in the face of trains). When they are all stopped...go back to the beginning of this paragraph.

When you have regained composure, go through your trains; familiarize yourself with each one, where it is, what it has, what it is supposed to be doing. Go through the maintenance work. Familiarize yourself with every authority, where it is, when it expires. Compare every authority with what you know, and if the territory is CTC, what you see.

Get out of the chair one more time. Walk to the coffeepot, walk to the restroom, walk outside but get away from it for a few minutes. If you have pushed too far and go right back to it, you'll just dig yourself in again.

Recognize what just happened and don't let it happen again. That's not easy to do. It's easy to try to be more of a hero than you can be. It's hard to say you've reached your limit.

The train dispatcher has ultimate control of the situation. When you can't follow each procedure correctly, can't keep up with the information and requests, don't know what is going on it is time to say no to more trains and no to more maintenance work.

The alternative to this advice: rules violations, derailments, collisions, injuries, and deaths have vastly more dire consequences than knowing your limit and not crossing it.

17. COMMUNICATION

*"I hope you believe you understand what you think I said,
but I'm not sure you realize that what you've heard is not
what I meant."*

Richard Nixon

Communication is a significant part of the train dispatcher's duties. Dispatchers are constantly publishing, in addition to verbal or written instructions, information about planned train movements, incidents, conditions, and past events. The communication may be oral or written, but generally it is important or essential information. Each communication should be precise and clear, whether or not it is related to safe operation. Communication that is not related to safe operation is probably related to efficient, reliable, economical operation, all of which are also within the dispatcher's domain.

Automated systems remove much of the hazard from train movement instructions. Electronic control systems perform the safety checks before a signal called by the dispatcher will allow movement. Many of the systems of train movement by written instructions provide a check of train movements before a document authorizing the use of a main track can be produced. The need to convey instructions verbally is the important weak point of these systems. In the case of electronic control systems, verbal communication is required for equipment failure, functions not within the capability of the system, and the use of main tracks by maintenance forces. In the case of written instruction systems, verbal communication often must be used to transmit the information from the dispatcher's copy of the document to the recipient's copy of the document.

WORKING WITH PEOPLE

Copying from the dispatcher is not an easy task for many train service and maintenance of way employees. They are generally copying under poor conditions: in a phone booth, in a locomotive cab, in the driver's seat behind the wheel with the document on the dashboard or in their lap or on the steering wheel or on the passenger seat. They are probably holding a microphone in one hand, holding the document with an elbow and writing with the other hand. It is an ancillary part of the job, not the reason for the job as had been the case with operators, and they are not specifically trained or equipped for the task. Some of them feel intimidated by their inability to keep up and may write the expected responses in advance in order to eliminate the problem of keeping up. Dispatchers are often their own worst enemy in this regard. They must keep up with an immense workload that just doesn't have time for people that need for them to send slow. Some will prove the fears of the intimidated to be correct when they blast through the authority at 70 words a minute and when the person copying doesn't get it right, chastise and/or ridicule before resending. The first essential is to remain within the ability of the person copying. It is generally a requirement of the rules and it is certainly common sense. The dispatcher did not establish the workload of the job. The people needing authority from the dispatcher to do their jobs didn't either and there is no reason to make them pay for shortcomings that are not their responsibility. The only essential element is that the instructions sent by the dispatcher and the instructions received from the dispatcher are the same instructions.

The same principle applies to information that will not be written. Regardless of the workload and the temptation to talk as fast as possible in order to keep up. Emulating an auctioneer is not productive. Few people on the other end of the conversation are accustomed to talk at a fast rate. The audio quality of their communication equipment is often poor, and there is often background noise (live and/or in the communication equipment) competing with the words being spoken.

VOICE COMMUNICATION

Until relatively recently, train dispatchers conducted all of their business on a party line telephone intended for that purpose alone. The dispatcher had absolute control over the communication circuit. That control provided three very important benefits:
- dispatchers could conduct business without interruption or competing conversations,

- dispatchers could select the business to be handled at any time,
- everyone conducting business with the dispatcher could hear everyone else.

Most of the conversations on the dispatcher's telephone circuit were between the dispatcher and operators specially trained to handle train operation communication. The combination of dedicated communication and trained personnel handling the information presented a relatively small amount of error in communication and a very efficient use of the dispatcher's time.

Dispatchers now have an array of communication devices that generally do not produce the advantages of the older technology. Telephone conversations are conducted on a conventional dial telephone circuit that reaches the dispatcher through voice mail and/or a holding queue. Radio conversations are conducted on an open channel that is available for any purpose from yard operations to automated messages and announcing signal indications. Telephone conversations may also be conducted on an open radio channel in the field, connected to the dial telephone equipment by a combination of tones generated by the keypad of the radio.

Communication will remain inefficient and unnecessarily hazardous unless technology is implemented that will restore organized and effective communication. Each of the following areas of consideration applied to the dispatcher's party line telephone. These cautions are even more important when using the communication facilities now typically available to train dispatchers.

BE CAREFUL OF WHAT YOU SAY

More people than just the intended recipient can hear much of what a train dispatcher says. The dispatcher is generally not aware of the number of people who are listening to information or instructions. Issuing instructions or information without regard to who may hear the information can contribute to or cause problems ranging from lost productivity and delayed trains to property damage and injury.

BE CAREFUL OF HOW YOU SAY IT

Dispatchers issue verbal and written information almost constantly. Each verbal or written transmission of information should mean exactly what it says.

Dispatchers should assume that the communication will fail before the conversation is complete. Always construct verbal communication with the most restrictive portion first. A local freight is calling for authority to enter the main track at a hand throw switch and proceed west. The dispatcher wants the local to follow another train, 7901 West. If the instruction is phrased

> *Engine 531 enter the main track and proceed west follow-ing 7901 West*

there is a chance that only

> *Engine 531 enter the main track and proceed west.*

will be heard. The train crewmember repeats the instruction as received and the dispatcher doesn't hear it because the radio or telephone circuit has failed. The dispatcher is momentarily upset that Engine 531 didn't repeat what was said. Engine 531 repeats what was heard and assumes that the dispatcher has become busy with someone else.

The dispatcher can call attention to the important parts of a verbal communication through emphasis and timing.

> *After 7901 west passes, Engine 531 enter the main track at Industry and proceed west.*

May be perceived and remembered differently than

> *AFTER...*
> *...7901 west passes...*
> *...THEN....*

> *....Engine 531 enter the main track at Industry and proceed*
> *west.*

Perception and memory are very important.

Sometimes (mis)pronunciation can be a memory aid or helpful if station names are similar. This is important if authority including either of two similar sounding stations is reasonable or if the limits are different than the requested limits. Bearrrrrring instead of Baring is less likely to be confused with Berne when radio or telephone reception quality is poor. Some time later, Langgggg CAS ter may be remembered and cause another look at the authority when Lancaster would not.

CONSIDER WHEN THE INFORMATION WILL BE USED

The passage of time may alter the content of verbal instructions. For example, a train is clear of the main track at a hand throw switch where it has been performing local switching. A crewmember reports that the train is now ready to leave. The safety of the movement is not in question. The electrically locked switch makes entry into the main track perfectly safe. If a train is approaching on the main track, the switch will not unlock. For traffic control reasons, the dispatcher does not want the local freight to leave before an important through freight train passes. The local freight may delay the important through train. The dispatcher tells the crewmember

> *After 7901 west passes, Engine 531 enter the main track at*
> *Industry and proceed west.*

The dispatcher's responsibility has been fulfilled. The crewmember has received instructions that must be executed. Train dispatchers should always remember that they are dealing with people. People tend to act human. If 7901 West does not pass within a very short period of time, the crewmembers will be passing the time going over the work to be performed at the next station, getting a head start on timeslip preparation, discussing sports, reading a book or magazine or any number of other things, legitimate or not. After an extended period of time, perhaps after 10 minutes or 20 minutes, the crew may have second thoughts about just sitting there. The conversation in the engine cab may be something like:

> *When we get to Nextville, drop me off 10 cars short of the*
> *crossing and I'll make the cut. That ought to hold us short*
> *of the crossing when we get back together. That dispatcher*
> *did say we can go, right?*
>
> *Mmmmmm, yeah, that's what you told me, right?*
>
> *Yeah, I called just before coming out with the pickup*
> *and....yeah, he says we can go. I'll line us out.*

If the answer the dispatcher gives is not the answer that is desired or expected, care should be taken to ensure that the response does not contain the expected or desired response and a qualifier.

If 7901 west is within a minute or two or is certainly within sight or hearing, the response "After 7901 west passes, Engine 531 enter the main track at Industry and proceed west" is reasonable. If 7901 west cannot be seen or heard and cannot be for more than a few minutes, the instruction "Call me when you see 7901 West" will ensure that the qualifier is not lost to the expected or desired result.

LISTEN

Verbal transmission of written instructions is the most dangerous part of train dispatching. Train order procedures generally involved sending the same instruction to several parties at one time. The dispatcher was responsible for checking the accurate repeat of each operator copying the order. That is no different from current methods for issuing instructions. The difference is that train order procedures made every operator copying the order responsible for checking the repeat of each other operator copying the order. The difference is important. The difference is so important that the Rock Island railroad required dispatchers to have a second station copy any order that only needed a single address, like the running authority for an extra train.

Dispatchers send most authority documents verbally to a single person. There are often several people who can hear the transmission, but generally no others involved in the conversation. The entire responsibility for an error rests with the train dispatcher. The error may be obvious such as Shelby instead of Ledger in a track warrant, but it can also be subtle. In one instance, a track inspector was given authority with the eastern limit at Baring. He showed up at Berne, 29 miles away. Contributing factors were the quality of the radio communication and his pronunciation of the words, or accent as some might say.

Train order dispatchers were comfortable with checking a repeat while occasionally lining a CTC signal or handling some other momentary distraction. First, there were others checking the repeat as well. Second, generally everybody involved was trained in the particular type of verbal communication needed and in the hazards associated with transmitting written documents by voice. These conditions no longer exist. A dispatcher would be prudent to devote 100 percent attention to the repeat of written instructions, leaving even the smallest distracting tasks until afterward.

MAKE THEM LISTEN

Dispatchers transmitting train orders tested operators to ensure that they were listening to the repeat of each other operator. The procedure required the operators to repeat in a specific order, but a dispatcher might break an operator in the middle of the repeat and tell another to go on from there. Failure was not an option.

Whenever possible, dispatchers should change something in the text of the authority. The idea is to provide something the person copying does not expect. Train orders were very flexible in this regard. There were often several ways to accomplish the same thing. Form based, fill-in-the-blanks, train control is not as flexible. The dispatcher can change the order of the limits of non-directional authority from permit-to-permit/day-to-day. The distant limit of a directional authority can be a station short of the destination of the train, even if there is no traffic to generate the need for the short limit. Adding items does not serve the same purpose as the additional lines may just be copied onto an incorrect document.

One way to ensure that the people copying authority are listening is to bust a partly completed authority and start over. This is especially important if the dispatcher suspects that the person requesting the authority has already filled in the blanks, which some may do in an attempt to keep up with the speed at which the dispatcher sends. Each authority requires a unique number and corrections are not allowed. Dispatchers can make use of this:

> *Number 1103 to AB Charlie work on the main track between Al...oh Break! I screwed it up. We'll start over with a new one... this will be number...*

and wait right there for the ok or go ahead response.

The person that says

> *I'm ok dispatcher, you can go on with the other one*

probably had the authority made out ahead of time. Send slow, be understanding, and if you work the same territory regularly, remember who needs a little patience and who can copy like an operator.

COMMUNICATION EQUIPMENT

For over 100 years, communication was not hampered by the communication equipment. The dispatcher had one primary communication circuit. The circuit was arranged so that everyone involved with train movement could hear the same information. The dispatcher had the ability to select whom to talk to at any given time. If a maintenance of way crew had authority until 1130, figured on an important train at 1140, the dispatcher could select that maintenance of way crew from the many people on the telephone and clear the authority in a timely fashion.

Modern technology has unfortunately changed the situation for the worse. The dispatcher's primary communication instruments are the dial phone circuit and the radio. The dial phone circuit handles one call at a time. Calls to the dispatcher are sent to a first in first out queue. If the maintenance of way crew clears on time and wants to clear the authority for the 1140 train, they will wait in line like everybody else. If the dispatcher is expecting the maintenance of way crew to call at 1130 and clear the authority, the only course is to keep answering the phone and handling whatever comes up until the needed phone call has been connected. It is possible for the maintenance of way crew to be sitting next to the delayed train, trying to clear the authority so that the train can move.

Radio is the other primary means of communication. The nature of radio communication generally prevents everyone involved in train movement from hearing the same information. The dispatcher may have several base stations, each with a range of a few miles. It is not unusual for someone to repeatedly call for the dispatcher on the radio because they are unable to hear the radio activity on a distant part of the line and the activity on the dial telephone circuit. All they know is that the dispatcher "won't answer".

Desktop fax machines and computer printers provide two other means of reaching the dispatcher. The use of these machines can result in important information being buried in a pile of paper. It is easy for the paper generated by these machines to reach the unmanageable level. No one on the telephone or the radio can hear the communication that is occurring as the paper from these machines is being read, sorted, and handled. That aggravates their impatience with the dispatcher that "won't answer".

Dispatchers should consider these shortcomings of the communication system and mitigate them to the extent possible. Methods include patching the telephone and radio circuits together if the system allows it, and broadcasting on more than one base radio station at the same time. When doing this, the dispatcher must be very careful to comply with the rules and Federal regulations.

If clearing track maintenance authority on time is critical, when issuing the authority, advise the foreman to call on the train radio frequency instead of trying to use the dial phone.

18. RULES AND REGULATIONS

Railroad operations are governed by a very complex set of rules and regulations. Train dispatchers are governed by these rules and regulations. They are also responsible for implementing them and supervising compliance. Typically, train dispatcher candidates must pass a rigorous examination on the various rules before completing the preparatory coursework. The examination can take many hours and is graded only pass/fail. After the initial examination, dispatchers must pass generally biennial examinations that are not as rigorous as the initial test.

The rulebooks contain some rules regarding behavior on the job, such as the prohibition of working under the influence of drugs or alcohol. Generally the rules are mandatory procedures for operating a railroad. The rules are complicated because operating a railroad is complicated, regardless of relatively recent efforts to simplify it.

OPERATING RULES

The Operating Rules is the book that generally prescribes operating practices and employee requirements. It is commonly known as just "The Rulebook" or "The Rules". The rulebook includes a section that is like the employee manual at many businesses, stating the general requirements for employees: appearance, conduct, use of company property and credit, and required and prohibited activities. This section of a rulebook is generally straightforward and requires no discussion. The rest of a railroad rulebook is a manual of procedures for operating the railroad. Specific requirements and prohibitions are described for subjects such as:

- The use and meaning of hand signals, locomotive whistle signals, signs, flags, and lights,
- General train movements including how and when the main track may be used, how trains are operated on sidings and yard tracks, speeds required in certain situations, switching procedures, how cars are situated in trains, flag protection, and procedures governing road crossings,

- Radio procedures,
- Procedures governing the operation of switches,
- Procedures for operation under various systems of traffic control,
- Procedures for operation under various signal systems,
- Procedures for the use of main track by maintenance forces,
- Specific requirements and procedures for train service employees, engine service employees, yardmasters, train dispatchers, station agents and others,

OTHER RULEBOOKS

The operating rules are generally supplemented by other rulebooks containing information, rules and procedures specific to certain groups of employees. Train dispatchers supervise the activity of employees engaged in train operation or the use of the main tracks and are often required to be conversant with or qualified on the rulebooks applying to the various disciplines.

M OF W RULES

The operating rules may be published in a special edition for Maintenance of Way employees. The M of W rules may contain generally the same material found in the operating rules, but it may not contain some of the rules specific to train operation. The M of W rulebook will contain rules and procedures specific to Maintenance of Way activities such as

- Operation of maintenance of way vehicles,
- Procedures for protection of defective track,
- Procedures for inspection, maintenance, and repair of track.

CONTROL OPERATOR RULES

Control operators handle traffic control equipment and direct the movement of trains using interlocking, CTC or other signal equipment. They may or may not be train dispatchers. Train dispatchers generally operate CTC equipment, but in some areas the system is operated by an employee that is not a train dispatcher. Often, these employees move the trains as directed by the train dispatcher. The train dispatcher is also a control operator when handling CTC or interlocking equipment. Control operator rules contain rules and procedures specific to the operation of traffic control equipment.

TRAIN DISPATCHER RULES

The train dispatcher rules cover situations and conditions applicable only to train dispatchers. Train dispatcher rules may cover
* procedures for the transfer of responsibility at the beginning/end of a shift,
* specific wording to be used in instructions issued under various circumstances,
* procedures for the failure of signal and traffic control systems,
* procedures for train movement in severe weather,
* records.

TRAIN HANDLING RULES

Train handling rules generally cover the mechanics of train operation. They generally include
* detailed description of air brakes and procedures for use and testing,
* detailed procedures for locomotive operation,
* procedures for train operation in situations such as starting, stopping, uphill and downhill movement, mountain grades, and use of airbrakes with and without dynamic braking.

SAFETY RULES

Generally the safety rules book contains procedures, requirements, and prohibitions for general safety at work. The safety rules contain requirements such as don't leave debris where it is a tripping hazard, don't leave file drawers open, and be careful carrying hot coffee. The safety rules are straightforward and do not require explanation or examination.

TIMETABLE AND SPECIAL INSTRUCTIONS

The timetable once contained schedules that were the authority for train movement on main tracks. Generally, they no longer contain schedules. When they do, they are generally no longer authority for operation. The timetable still defines the railroad for operation and contains instructions that supplement or replace the operating rules. Timetables are numbered and show the date and time they are effective. There is only one timetable in effect for any part of the railroad at any time.

A railroad is divided into several units for management purposes and operating purposes. Depending upon the size of the railroad, the largest division may be a region or some similar unit. The region generally contains two or more divisions or similar units. Each division is divided into subdivisions or districts. Each district may have one or more named branch lines in addition to the main route. The timetable defines the entire organization. The timetable may be a single book for the entire railroad, for a region, or a division.

For railroad operation, a station is a single point designated by a sign adjacent to the track. A subdivision or district is generally a single route between two stations. The timetable lists each station on the subdivision and its location. The location is generally shown as a distance from one of the end stations of the subdivision or as a milepost location. Mileposts designate distance from a point generally associated with the original construction of the line. It is important to know that mileposts are not necessarily a mile apart. They may have been when the line was constructed, but alignment changes over the years may have lengthened or shortened the track between mileposts. Sometimes a complete reroute of the original line results in a point at which one or more miles are missing. Where the changes are relatively small, the mileposts remain as they were, but the distance between them is more or less than a mile. Locations measured in tenths of these miles are measured in tenths of the distance between the mileposts, not 528 foot tenths-of-a-mile. When the change is large, such as a line relocation that shortened the distance by miles, the measurements continue from the origin end along the new line to the point where it joins the original line. That point is known as an equation. Equations may be designated as MP 82.95=MP 93.0 or 82.95/93.0.

The timetable will not show the lengths of individual miles and may not show the location of equations. The track chart will often show the location of equations and may show the lengths of individual miles. Train dispatchers should be familiar with extraordinary-length miles and equations. When rules designate a distance requirement, such as flagging, track flag location, or restricting a train, the distance requirement is in 5280-foot miles. A serious error can be made if a train dispatcher is not aware of the unusual mileposts on the district.

Rail alignments are generally not a straight line between the endpoints of a subdivision or branch line. In mountainous areas, trains may operate for much of the trip in directions vastly different from the general direction between the endpoints, including the opposite direction. The alignment may be almost circular, with the front of a long train passing over or under the rear of the same train. The timetable designates the "timetable direction" for each subdivision and branch line, if routes are designated in that manner. The timetable direction need not represent the general direction between the endpoints, or even a compass direction. One end of the subdivision may be directly north of the other end of the subdivision, yet the directions will be East and West for consistency with other subdivisions of the same railroad. In a terminal area, the directions may be Inbound and Outbound.

The timetable shows whether stations have one or more sidings and the length of the sidings. It also shows stations on multiple track lines that have crossovers. It generally contains other information specific to train operation on the subdivision such as radio channels, speed limits, operating rules in effect, and specific car or locomotive restrictions.

The timetable may also contain modifications and additions to the operating rules. Generally, the modifications have been made because the operating rules do not apply to a situation unique to the specific railroad or specific local area. For example, the rulebook may state that unattended cars must have a sufficient number of handbrakes applied to prevent movement. The time-table may specify handbrakes and wheel chocks or skates for unattended cars at a station or on a specific track because of the steep grade. The modifications may also be permanent changes that will be carried in the timetable until a new rulebook is issued. It is very important to remember that operating rules changes in the timetable are additional rules, not replacements or changes to existing rules unless the timetable changes specifically states that it is a modification or replacement.

The timetable may be published in two separate volumes: the timetable and the special instructions. The timetable book will generally contain only the station information, the directions, sidings and crossovers. The special instructions will contain the other information. The timetable of a large railroad may also have a third volume, the System Special Instructions. The Special Instructions applies locally and the System Special Instructions contains information that applies anywhere on the company's lines.

GENERAL ORDERS, BULLETINS, AND NOTICES

Conditions often change more frequently than timetables can be reissued. General Orders, Bulletins, Notices and similar publications are a short-term method of publication of the same type of special instructions that are found in the timetable. As with operating rules modifications found in the timetable, instructions in these documents only replace other rules and instructions when it is specifically stated in the text of the instruction. A General Order, Bulletin, or Notice is in effect until it is cancelled by another. Instructions in General Orders, Bulletins, or Notices are in effect simultaneously and do not modify the content of another General Order, Bulletin, or Notice unless it is specifically stated in the instruction.

New General Orders, Bulletins, or Notices may be published on a frequent basis. They are generally posted on a clipboard or in a binder known as a bulletin board or bulletin book. Each train dispatching office generally has a bulletin board or book. They are also generally located at terminals where train crews report for duty.

Train dispatchers must check the bulletin book for new information at the beginning of every shift. The reference timetable at the dispatcher's desk and the dispatcher's personal copy of the timetable should be marked with all current revisions to ensure that nothing is overlooked.

REGULATIONS

In the US, railroad operation is regulated by the Federal Railroad Administration of the US Department of Transportation. The regulations are contained in the Code of Federal Regulations Title 49 parts 200-299. This volume is very important to train dispatchers. The regulations include Hours of Service, Locomotive Inspection, Track Safety Standards, Workplace Safety and many other areas that come under the direct control of the train dispatcher. Fines for violation of the regulations may be levied against individual employees.

The regulations are cited by Title, Part, and Section. Section 7 of the track Safety Standards is cited as 49 CFR 213.7. The railroad operating regulations, Title 49, are available as a book from the US Government Bookstore. Branches of the store are located in several large cities throughout the US. Books may also be purchased at the online US Government Bookstore http://bookstore.gpo.gov/.

WHAT DO THEY ALL MEAN?

There are several reasons for not using an introductory work for a detailed study of the rules and regulations that apply to train dispatchers. The two most important are:
- It would be overwhelming to a beginner,
- There are several different rulebooks in effect throughout the country. Rules from the same book may be applied differently by different railroads. A comprehensive course would also be confusing to a beginner.

Instead, this chapter will explore how to read the rules and generally interpret them.

Railroad operation is complex. The complexity cannot be avoided. The method of examining the rules that is described in the example at the end of this chapter breaks the study down to a level that is easier to understand than attempting to comprehend a book full of complex and interrelated rules by just reading them cover-to-cover or even one complete rule at a time.

MEMORIZING

Some methods may emphasize memorization techniques and the ability to recite certain rules by rote. That method works reasonably well for studying to pass an examination. It may not work well when an individual is confronted with an unusual situation that must be handled correctly. Knowing the contents of the rules and regulations and understanding them may seem like an impossible task, but it is not. Information that one uses regularly and understands is much easier to retain than information one doesn't understand and is only attempting to have available for recall as it is written.

JUST WHAT THEY SAY

Never "read anything in" to rules or regulations. They mean exactly what they say, and no more. A good approach is to read each as if it were a foreign language and it is necessary to look up each word in a translating dictionary. In some cases, a poorly written rule or regulation may seem ambiguous when read carefully in this manner. If this occurs, an interpretation is necessary. Each railroad has designated officers who are authorized to provide interpretations in these cases. The question should be submitted in writing and an answer should be expected in writing to ensure that there is no mistake or misunderstanding.

Many terms used in rules and regulations have an exact meaning. Understanding the application and context of the words is essential to understanding the requirements of the rule or regulation. Rulebooks generally contain a section of definitions of terms. The definitions are a good place to begin learning, since understanding of the rules relies upon understanding the words used in the rules. Analyze each rule in the manner described in the previous pages.

IN EFFECT SIMULTANEOUSLY

Unless specifically stated otherwise, each instruction, rule, and regulation is unaffected by others. All, unless specifically stated, are in effect simultaneously. The exception may be made by being specified:

...modifies the provisions of rule...

or

...except as provided by rule...

The exception may also be made by grouping rules:

RULES IN EFFECT IN CTC TERRITORY

In the latter case, the rules that specifically apply to CTC territory are in effect in CTC Territory. Rules that do not specifically apply to CTC territory are in effect. Rules that apply only to another traffic control system are not in effect.

The same concept applies to speed. The popular interpretation "the most restrictive one is in effect" is not correct. Again, they are all in effect. If the speed limit zone is 60 m.p.h. and defective track causes a 30 m.p.h. speed restriction, both speed limits are in effect at the same time. A train moving at 30 m.p.h. is not exceeding 30 m.p.h. It is also not exceeding 60 m.p.h. If the train has a car restricted to 40 m.p.h., it is not exceeding 60 m.p.h. at the same time as it is not exceeding 40 m.p.h. As it moves through the defective track, moving at 30 m.p.h. does not exceed 40 m.p.h. or 60 m.p.h.

The application of time in railroad operation has been greatly reduced, but the same principle applies to time. If a train has authority that is not in effect until 0830 and it also has an instruction to not leave the initial station before 0845, both are in effect. Before 0830 both restrictions are in effect. The train must not leave until 0830. It must also not leave until 0845. At 0830 the restriction on its authority has been fulfilled and only the 0845 restriction is in effect. The application of the principle to time was an essential component of timetable and train order operation. The application of the principle to time in current operations is unusual.

Simultaneous application of all rules and instructions is important when changing a single instruction. If the timetable restricts all trains handling 40 foot flat cars to 30 m.p.h., an instruction issued to restrict car ABCD 201, a 40 foot flat car, to 40 m.p.h. will result in the train moving at 30 m.p.h. If the desired effect is to move ABCD 201 at 40 m.p.h., the instruction must specifically except car ABCD 201 from the timetable instruction.

Correct:

CAR ABCD 201 MUST BE HANDLED NOT EXCEEDING 40 MPH INSTEAD OF 30 MPH ON TIMETABLE SPECIAL INSTRUCTION 302.

The instruction must apply to the car, not to the train.

Incorrect:

DO NOT EXCEED 40 MPH INSTEAD OF 30 MPH ON TIMETABLE SPECIAL INSTRUCTION 302 WHILE HANDLING CAR ABCD 201

Worded that way, the instruction limiting 40 foot flatcars to 30 m.p.h. is changed while handling ABCD 201 regardless of other 40 foot flat cars in the train. Train dispatchers must be extremely cautious whenever issuing an instruction that reduces the restriction on a train.

A similar situation can arise when excepting a special high speed train from the speed limits that normally apply. If the maximum freight train speed is 60 m.p.h. and a special freight train may operate at passenger train speed not exceeding 70 m.p.h., an instruction

> DO NOT EXCEED 70 MPH INSTEAD OF 60 MPH

Would unintentionally authorize the freight train to operate at 70 m.p.h. where passenger trains are restricted to 60 m.p.h. The instruction should be specific.

> PASSENGER TRAIN SPEED LIMITS INSTEAD OF FREIGHT TRAIN SPEED LIMITS APPLY TO 1234 WEST.

If the high speed freight train cannot exceed 70 m.p.h., the instruction would read

> PASSENGER TRAIN SPEED LIMITS NOT EXCEEDING 70 MPH INSTEAD OF FREIGHT TRAIN SPEED LIMITS APPLY TO 1234 WEST

Or

> PASSENGER TRAIN SPEED LIMITS INSTEAD OF FREIGHT TRAIN SPEED LIMITS APPLY TO 1234 WEST.
>
> DO NOT EXCEED 70 MPH

Before issuing instructions, formulate the wording and consider it carefully. Does the wording unintentionally remove any restrictions on the operation of the train?

EXAMPLE

This example was drawn from an edition of a rulebook used by several North American railroads. This example explores how to read the rules and determine what they mean. It does not directly explain the meaning of the rules. Since the explanation applies to method and not meaning or interpretation, it is appropriate for general application.

The subject is a single rule (10.1) governing entry into CTC limits. Rule 10.1 is a subheading of rule 10.0, so that is the place to start.

> ## 10.0 Rules Applicable Only in Centralized Traffic Control (CTC)

The rules in section 10 apply only in Centralized Traffic Control. All other rules except those specifically designated as exclusive to some other type of operation are also in effect simultaneously.

> ## 10.1 Authority to Enter CTC Limits

Rule 10 applies only in CTC. This rule applies specifically to entering CTC limits. What is CTC?

> ### CTC
>
> See Centralized Traffic Control.
>
> ### Centralized Traffic Control (CTC)
>
> A block system that uses block signal indications to authorize train movements.

CTC is a Block System. What is a Block System?

> ### Block System
>
> A block or series of consecutive blocks within ABS, ACS, CTC, or interlocking limits.

This definition refers to CTC, where we started. Don't be confused by the apparent redundancy. We are examining CTC and the definition includes CTC. What is a block?

> **Block**
>
> A length of track:
> * between consecutive block signals.
> * between a block signal and the end of block system limits.
> * or
> * in ATC limits the use of which is governed by cab signals and/or block signals.

Since we want to know, right now, about how a block relates to CTC, ignore the reference to ATC. The definition of a block is dependent on the definition of Block Signals. What are Block Signals?

> **Block Signal**
>
> A fixed signal at the entrance of a block that governs trains entering and using that block.

We have determined that a block is a length of track between consecutive block signals or between a block signal and the end of block system limits. The block signal governs trains entering and using the block. The combination of definitions is self-referencing, but straightforward. A block is a length of track. It is delimited by block signals. Block signals govern trains entering or using the block. What is a fixed signal?

> **Fixed Signal**
>
> A signal that is fixed to a location permanently and that indicates a condition affecting train movement.

A fixed signal is a signal, whatever that is, fixed to a location. It indicates a condition affecting train movement. The fixed signal governs trains entering and using the block and it indicates a condition affecting train movement. Whether or not a train may use a block is a condition affecting train movement. Now; what is a signal?

A definition of signal is not provided. Signal, is used as is common in the railroad industry. There is no special meaning for this term; however, it is not limited to a mast with lights. A fixed signal may be a sign, a flag, or a special device such as a switch target.

The term train has been used repeatedly. These definitions are connected to the definition of a train. What is a train?

Train

One or more engines coupled, with or without cars, displaying a marker, and authorized to operate on a main track. A term that when used in connection with speed restrictions, flag protection, and the observance of all signals and signal rules also applies to engines.

A train must first be an engine. An engine is:

Engine

A unit propelled by any form of energy or more than one of these units operated from a single control. Engines are used in train or yard service. Rules that apply to engines also apply to cab control cars.

This definition could be tricky. Some railroad equipment may not be what it seems when the definition is applied. That is why the definitions must be applied carefully when interpreting the rules. One variation of an old question on operating rules interpretation asks

> *What is a flatcar, moved by a donkey on a treadmill on the car, while it is being used to switch cars in the yard?*

It is an Engine

Many years ago there was little confusion. When self-propelled cranes began to be used in maintenance of way service, the line was blurred. If the self-propelled crane is pulling cars used in the maintenance work, is it an engine? That became a matter of interpretation for individual railroads. The problem is now more complex. A machine that looks like a diesel locomotive and probably had been used as a diesel locomotive at one time, may now be used to move equipment used in repairing and maintaining track. In this context, it is probably not an engine, since the track equipment itself is not used in train or yard service. Thus, the track maintenance equipment is not an engine.

There are other vehicles that look like conventional highway trucks that are equipped to move railroad cars. These vehicles are equipped with standard railroad couplers and airbrake equipment. If the vehicle is switching cars in a yard or pulling a revenue train, it obviously meets the definition of an Engine. If it is pulling cars used by maintenance of way forces during the course of maintenance work, the distinction is not clear, as with the self-propelled crane. If there is any question of whether a vehicle is an engine for a specific circumstance, the dispatcher should apply in writing to an officer authorized to provide rules interpretations.

Having determined that an engine is involved, the other elements of the definition must be explored. To be a train it must have a marker. This is a little confusing to a beginner. There is no definition of a marker in the definitions. The definition of a marker is contained in the rule about markers.

5.10 Markers

A marker of the prescribed type must be displayed on the trailing end of the rear car to indicate the rear of the train.

We won't follow the train of the prescribed types of marker. The information in this rule is what is needed at the moment. A marker indicates the rear of a train. The first two elements of the definition of a train indicate that it must have an engine and it must have a marker. The definition of a marker indicates that it is part of a train. The third part of the definition says that in addition to the other two elements, it must be authorized to operate on a main track. What is a main track?

Main Track

A track extending through yards and between stations that must not be occupied without authority or protection.

The definition of a main track also refers to authority. As a matter of simplicity, we won't follow the path to the protection part of the definition. It isn't relevant at the moment. There is no definition for authority. The rule on the next page explains how it is obtained, however. For simplicity, we won't look into protection. The method is the same as has been followed to this point.

6.3 Main Track Authorization

Do not occupy main tracks unless authorized by one of the following:

- Rule 6.13 (Yard Limits)
- Rule 6.14 (Restricted Limits) Rule 6.15 (Block Register Territory)
- Rule 9.14 (Movement with the Current of Traffic)
- Rule 9.15 (Track Permits)
- Rule 10.1 (Authority to Enter CTC Limits)
- Rule 14.1 (Authority to Enter TWC Limits)
- Rule 14.6 (Movement Against the Current of Traffic)
- Rule 15.3 (Authorizing Movement Against the Current of Traffic)
- Rule 16.1 (Authority to Enter DTC Limits)
- At manual interlockings, verbal authority from the control operator or a controlled signal that indicates proceed.
- Special instructions or general order. When unable to obtain authority and it is necessary to foul or occupy a main track in ABS, protection must be provided in both directions as outlined under Rule 9.17.1 (Signal Protection in ABS by Lining Switch).

Written authorities that are no longer in effect must be retained until the end of tour of duty, unless otherwise instructed by the train dispatcher.

Tracing all of the terms in the title of the rule, we find that we are back to the contents of the same rule. The excursion hasn't been wasted, however. We now understand that

- CTC is a block system.
- CTC uses block signal indications to authorize movements.
- Blocks are delimited by signals that govern the use of the blocks.
- Signal indications apply to trains.
- A train must have an engine, a marker and authority to use a main track.

- A main track must not be occupied without authority or protection.

From this information we know that signal indications do not apply to maintenance of way equipment, since maintenance of way equipment does not meet the definition of an engine. Since signal indications do not apply to maintenance of way equipment, it is not possible for maintenance of way equipment to be authorized by signal indications. Since authority or protection is required, there must be another method of authorizing occupancy of main tracks by other than trains.

(10.1 continued)

CTC limits are designated in the timetable. Sidings within CTC limits are controlled sidings and are governed by CTC rules. A train must not enter or occupy any track where CTC is in effect unless:

The rules in section 10 apply only in CTC territory. The timetable specifies the limits of CTC. Also, sidings in CTC are controlled sidings. What is a siding?

Siding

A track connected to the main track and used for meeting or passing trains. Location of sidings are shown in the timetable.

A track needs two things to be a siding. It must be used for meeting and passing of trains and it must be shown in the timetable. Lacking either, it is not a siding. The rule states that if a siding is within CTC limits, it is a controlled siding. What is a controlled siding?

Controlled Siding

A siding within CTC or interlocking limits where a signal indication authorizes the siding's use.

Rule 10.1 states that all sidings in CTC are controlled sidings.

Rules that apply to sidings do not apply to tracks not used for meeting and passing of trains regardless of the presence of a controlled signal governing entrance to the track.

A track that is not designated in the timetable as a siding and is not a main track cannot meet the requirements of CTC limits.

If a track in CTC limits is a siding, it must be governed by signal indication.

Only trains and engines can be authorized by signal indication. Engines are included because the definition of a train includes engines for the application of signal rules. For the experienced, one can argue at length about whether the rules being quoted actually allow an engine to be authorized by signal indication in CTC. This is not, however, an area of exploration for the novice.

(10.1 continued)

- A controlled signal displays a proceed indication.

The signal that authorizes entry into CTC limits must be a controlled signal. What is a controlled signal?

Controlled Signal

An absolute signal controlled by a control operator.

To be a controlled signal, it must be an absolute signal. What is an absolute signal?

Absolute Signal

A block or interlocking signal without a number plate, or designated by an A marker.

For simplicity, we will not consider the part of the definition that leads us away from the CTC rule being considered. An absolute signal is a block signal. Block signals are found in tracking down the definition of CTC. The trail to the number plate is not as straightforward as some of the exploration. The number plate and A marker are not covered in the definitions. They are found in the signal aspects and indications rules. What is a signal aspect?

> **Signal Aspect**
>
> The appearance of a fixed or cab signal.

This definition causes us to look toward signal aspects rules for clarification. These rules have pictures representing each aspect that can be displayed by a signal. In these pictures, the number plate or A marker if used will be seen.

> *(10.1 continued)*
> or
> •   Verbal authority is granted as follows:

Here we find that there is a way to authorize entry into CTC territory other than signal indications.

> *(10.1 continued)*
>
> The control operator authorizes movement past a Stop indication under Rule 9.12.1 (CTC Territory).

The first method involves rule 9.12.1, which says:

9.12.1 CTC Territory

At a signal displaying a Stop indication, if no conflicting movement is evident, the train will be governed as follows:

- A crew member must immediately contact the control operator, unless the train is:

Control operator is mentioned in the definition of controlled signal and here. What is a control operator?

Control Operator

Employee assigned to operate a CTC or interlocking control machine or authorized to grant track permits.

The definition is straightforward. The rules don't provide a definition of a CTC or interlocking control machine. As in the definition of a signal, the commonly accepted use of the term control machine is accepted. Track permits are not relevant to the exploration of this rule, so it will be ignored for this discussion.

(9.12.1 continued)

- Within track and time limits

There is no definition for track and time limits. Later in this rule, 10.3 is cited. It says

10.3 Track and Time

The control operator may authorize a train to occupy a track or tracks within specified limits for a certain time period. Authority must include track designation, track limits, and time limit. The train may use the track in either direction within the specified limits until the limits are verbally released.

Limits designated by a switch extend only to the signal governing movement over the switch unless otherwise designated.

This rule does not state that the authority described is verbal authority. It is implied by the information that must be included in the authority. The rule applies to trains. Anything that does not meet the definition of a train cannot be authorized to enter CTC limits with this rule.

(9.12.1 continued)

or

- Entering track and time limits from any point other than either end of track and time limits.

Before authorizing the train to proceed, the control operator must know that the route is properly lined and no conflicting movement is occupying or authorized to enter the track between that signal and the next absolute signal governing movement or the end of CTC where applicable.

When the train receives these instructions, "After stopping, (train) at (location) has authority to pass signal displaying Stop indication," specifying the route where applicable, the train must move at restricted speed.

For simplicity, we will not move from here to an examination of track and time. This example shows how to examine the rules in order to understand them. Taking the path too far from the rule being examined will cause the inexperienced to be confused. We have discovered what Track and Time is, which is sufficient for the moment.

The control operator authorizes the train to enter tracks between block signals by stating, "(Train) at (location) has authority to enter (track) and proceed (direction)." After entering the track, the train is authorized to move only in the direction specified.

Here is another method of authorizing a train to enter CTC limits verbally. Thus far, we haven't found a way to authorize something that is not a train.

(10.1 continued)

or

- The control operator grants track and time under Rule 10.3 (Track and Time).

Here is a method that, so far, isn't limited to trains. Simplifying again, let's look at rule 10.3. Looking through rule 10.3, we find the method for authorizing something that is not a train to enter CTC limits.

10.3.2 Protection of Machines, Track Cars, or Employees

Machines, track cars, or employees will receive track and time in the same manner as trains.

Machines, track cars, or employees must be clear of the limits before the employee granted track and time releases the authority.

The method discussed in this chapter can be used to continue examining Rule 10.0 and its subheadings, the rest of the operating rules, the special instructions, the federal regulations, and the other rules and instructions that apply to railroad operation.

Remember the two important principles
- Read what is written - *only* what is written - word for word,
- All rules, instructions, and regulations are in effect simultaneously unless the wording of an individual item specifically states otherwise.

19. TOOLS AND REFERENCES

CRUTCH

Knowing running times for all types of trains between any two points on the district is essential. Often an experienced dispatcher will provide a student or an experienced dispatcher learning a new territory with a crutch for the territory. A crutch gives running times between stations for various types of trains for the territory. It also generally gives the length of call figure (the amount of advance notice) required for terminal stations and the straight running time location of a train that is the call figure amount of time away from the terminal. A simple example crutch is shown in Fig. 15-4 page 72.

TRACK CHART

A **TRACK CHART**, also called a **CONDENSED PROFILE**, is a schematic map or diagram of the railroad. It shows track arrangement and generally shows mileposts, location of stations, location and degree of curve, location and percent of grade, bridges, tunnels, speed limits (the amount of detail varies). It may also show other important information such as

- road crossings,
- signals,
- signal system in effect,
- operating rules in effect,
- type, size, and age of rail,
- type, size and last maintenance of ties,
- last maintenance of ballast,
- culverts.

Each dispatching position should have a track chart of the territory available for immediate reference. When possible, train dispatchers should obtain a personal copy of the track charts for territory being worked, and keep on it any notes and personal reminders about the characteristics of the territory.

Parts of typical track charts are shown on the following pages.

TRACK CHART COMMENT LEGEND

A   Track Arrangement

B   Grade

C   Elevation

D   Alignment (curves)

E   Type of Operation (CTC, TWC, DTC, Yard Limits, etc.)

F   Signal Location

G   Turnout Size (No 11, No 20, etc.)

H   Road Crossings

I   Distance Equation (if any occur)

J   Elevation Equation (if any occur)

K   Survey Stations (accurate distances in feet in the format 0+00 - hundreds of feet + feet - from specific starting points with an equation where starting point has changed (e.g. 9800+55=3+90)

L   Length of Miles (in feet)

M   Speed Limit

N   Maintenance History (type and age of rail, ballast, last tie replacement and surfacing, and so on)

O   Bridges, Tunnels, Culverts

P   Construction Date

Q   Mile Post

R   Right of Way

S   Track Maintenance Supervisor

T   Pole Line

U   Station Sign Location

V   Siding Length

W   Slide Fences

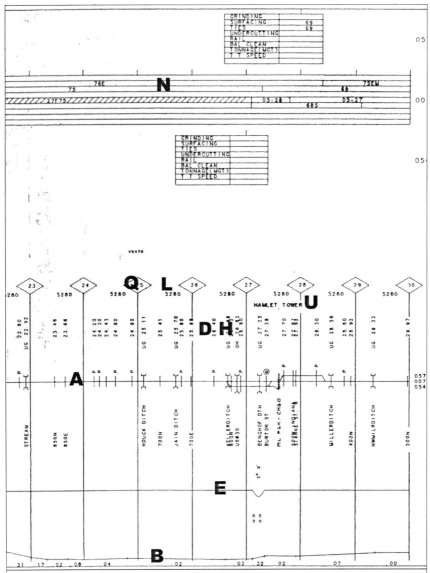

Fig. 19-1 The standards for track charts vary widely among railroads and even in different eras on the same railroad. As this and the following examples show, the amount of information included varies greatly. The manner in which the information is represented is sufficiently similar to allow correct interpretation of an unfamiliar format. This track chart contains only a small amount of information, some of which is only partially represented, such as the station location (U) that does not include the milepost location of the station.

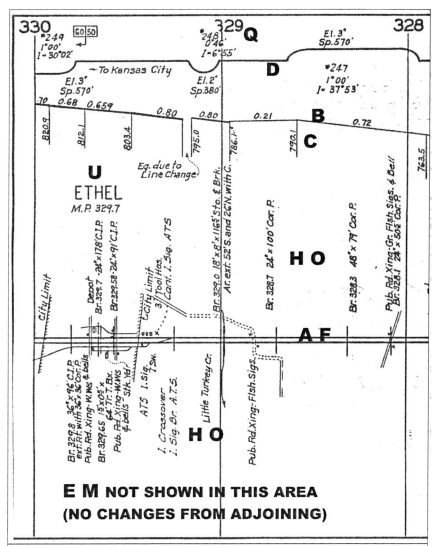

Fig. 19-2 Some track charts, such as Fig. 19-1 are drawn in a very small scale, which is not objectionable if the detail of the information shown is limited. Others are drawn to a very large scale, allowing the information that is shown to be read easily. In this example, more detail is shown than in Fig. 19-1, but information that can be important to train dispatchers (e.g. length of sidings, length of miles) is missing. The curve symbols (D) look like they should represent which way the track would curve if one were standing on the track line looking toward the symbol, but they do not. The curved sections are on the same side of the tangent line as the center of the curve (the opposite of what would seem correct), which is typical on track charts.

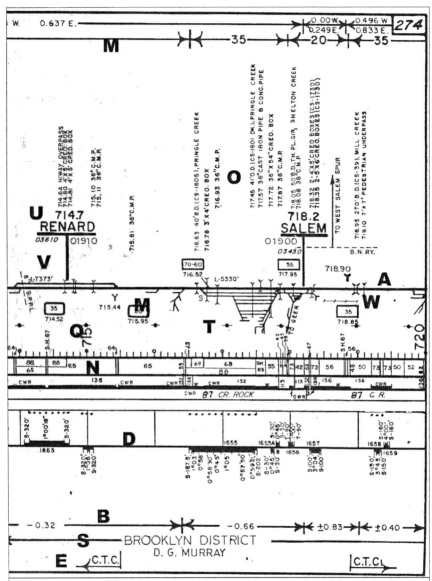

Fig. 19-3 This track chart contains more information and greater detail than Fig. 19-1 or 19-2. Some of the symbols are different, but are sufficiently similar to those in the previous examples to allow accurate interpretation. (e.g. the curves are represented by a heavy line rather than a curved line, but still on the side toward the center of the curve). Actual location of speed limit signs is shown (M) as is the practice in Fig. 19-2, but the entire length of each speed limit zone is shown at the top of the page.

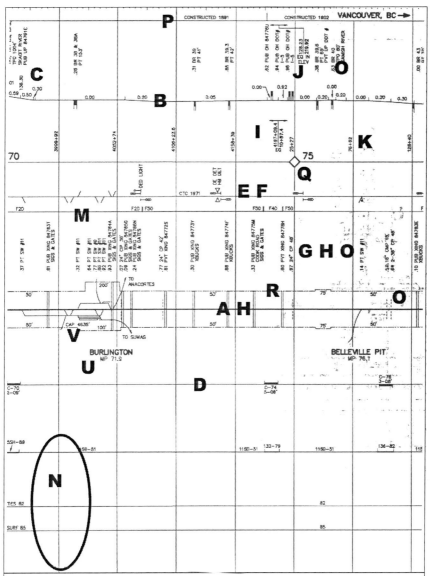

Fig. 19-4 Some track charts have a great amount of information and great detail about each item. This track chart contains much more information than the previous examples. Much of what is also contained in the other examples is described in greater detail. Although the length of each mile is not shown, survey stationing is shown, allowing the length of any mile to be calculated easily. For example, MP 74 is at station 4158+39. MP 73 is at station 4106+23.6. The length of the mile is 415,839 (feet from the origin) - 410,623.6 (feet from the origin) = 5215.4 feet.

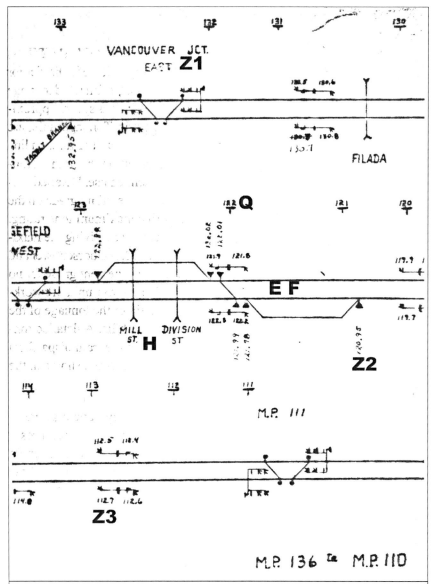

Fig. 19-5 Train dispatchers often supplement the information that the engineering department provides on the track charts. The additional information may be gained by field observation or by advice from train crews and maintenance of way personnel. This diagram includes (Z1) CTC control point names, (Z2) location of electric lock switches, and (Z3) signal locations, indications displayed on each signal, and automatic block signal numbers.

TONNAGE TABLE

A **TONNAGE TABLE (TONNAGE CHART, TONNAGE RATING)** gives the maximum possible tonnage on a district or portion of a district for each locomotive type. A locomotive pulling a train that is full rated tonnage for a district will travel at the minimum practical continuous speed (approximately twelve mph) when it encounters the ruling grade. Tonnage tables are helpful and may be essential in the case of a locomotive unit failure, on line work, or **SLEEPERS** (cars not shown on the train list) in the train. A tonnage table can sometimes work in reverse of its intended use. Detailed tonnage tables may give a hint of train performance on the ruling grade on the line by comparing train tonnage to the locomotive maximum tons rating. Some tonnage tables can improve prediction accuracy by giving the maximum tonnage rating at several speeds. If a train with 12,000 horsepower and 4,000 tons is moving at twenty mph on a continuous 1 percent grade for no apparent reason (the engineer says that all of the locomotive units are working properly), there are probably sleepers in the train or the tonnage of the cars is significantly different than shown on the waybills. A detailed tonnage chart (and / or the experience of the engineer or the train dispatcher) can lead to an estimate of the tonnage and number of cars not shown in the train list.

Some railroads do not use tonnage tables. Instead they have a standard horsepower per ton ratio for each district. Generally, a train requires 1 horsepower per ton per each percent of grade to ensure making the grade without stalling. The characteristics of individual locomotives may allow them to pull more tonnage than the formula result and severe weather may limit the tonnage that can be handled. Generally, this is a safe figure if there is no tonnage table available.

LABOR AGREEMENTS

Train dispatchers are frequently required to instruct train or engine crew members or maintenance of way employees on what work to perform, or when and where to perform work. A train dispatcher's instruction may violate the provisions of a labor agreement, or cause a penalty payment. Train dispatchers should have a good understanding of the provisions of labor agreements for employees they supervise while on or subject to work on the main tracks including trainmen, engineers, signal maintainers, and track maintenance forces. Credibility is important when working with or supervising people. After making a decision and instructing a crew to do something that could cause a penalty payment, stand behind the decision. If the penalty timeslip is sent to you for verification or approval, approve it. If it is not and the crew later complains about having the claim rejected, notify the authority rejecting the claim that it is valid, explaining the circumstances as necessary. Do not attempt to avoid trouble for yourself by denying that you issued the instruction.

HAZARDOUS MATERIAL PROCEDURE BOOKS

Each train dispatching office should be equipped with one or more books that no dispatcher ever wants to use and all must be familiar with. The hazardous material emergency response books give the emergency procedures to follow if there is a release of any type of hazardous material. Many railroad information systems have inquiries for retrieval of hazardous material emergency handling instructions by car number and/or commodity. Never, under any circumstances, rely only on information contained in that system. If there is a derailment and a hazardous material release, life may depend upon immediate action. If the response from the system is immediate, use the information it provides. The computer system may be down or very slow to respond, however. Know how to look up hazardous material in the books quickly by commodity. Know how to read and understand the instructions. Part of a slow night, weekend, or holiday shift would be well spent periodically going over the hazardous material procedures to maintain familiarity. There will be little time to spend figuring out the manuals when a derailed car is leaking or on fire.

The hazardous material handling regulations (normal procedures, not emergency response instructions) is another important, but less urgent, work that should be in the dispatcher's office and / or may be excerpted in the timetable or special instructions . Train dispatchers should be familiar with this material, particularly the documentation requirements and the required location in the train of hazardous material cars. If a train crew reports a misplaced hazardous material car in the train or missing documents, make sure you know the requirements before issuing instructions. Never instruct a train to proceed with improperly placed hazardous material cars or without the required documentation.

20. REMEMBER, MEMORIZE...AND DON'T RELY ON MEMORY

Train dispatchers must remember a vast amount of information. They must also memorize a vast amount of information. The two are different. The difference is important.

REMEMBERING

If you are driving on the highway and pass a 45 m.p.h. speed limit sign, you do not memorize the sign. You don't use methods involving clues or association. You simply train yourself to remember that the last speed limit sign was 45 m.p.h. Signs are posted along the road to refresh the memory as well as inform drivers who have entered the road and not yet passed a speed limit sign. If you do not regularly travel the road, remembering the speed limit as you drive is valuable. Memorizing the speed limit is not. Once you pass a speed limit sign that shows a different speed limit, you must remember the new current speed limit. You have no need to remember the previous speed limit. If you travel the same route regularly, you will memorize the speed limits not because of a memorization exercise, but because you use the information repeatedly.

The information a train dispatcher must remember is approached similarly to the speed limit signs along the road. In general terms, a train dispatcher must know what is going on. That's a tall order. There are several trains; some early, some late, some with work, some without. Some trains may have insufficient power to make the usual speed, some have a crew with limited time remaining on the hours of service, and there may be a crew that never makes the usual time regardless of the size of train and amount of power. There are maintenance workers changing ties, changing rails, surfacing, maintaining signals and any number of other maintenance activities. All of this information plays a part in planning and in response to unexpected events. Knowing what is supposed to happen is also an essential factor in recognizing the unexpected.

A train dispatcher should review all of the activity on the territory frequently. When not planning, issuing authority, or making records, and other functions that require attention, review

- The trains, current and pending. Review the power, the crew, the consist, the station work, figures that you have published or have been given to you, instructions on train handling, the authority that the train has, the current location, the expected location, where and when it will encounter other trains, and anything else known about each train.
- Track maintenance forces, current and pending. Review who has been authorized to work on the main track, where, for how long, and the work being performed. Review pending work. Who was told to call after which trains, who has work to do that doesn't fit into the picture now but may if something changes. Review the possible effects of the work. Some activities such as tie replacement or ballasting will result in a slow order when the work is complete. Rail replacement and ballast work often results in repairs to signal wires that must be completed after the scheduled work is complete.
- The general condition of the railroad. Review the slow orders for location, speed and effect on trains. If the weather is severe, review the last reports and consider the time that has elapsed since. Review the instructions in the live file.

MEMORIZING

Train dispatchers must memorize, or commit to memory, a large volume of non-dynamic information. The content of many operating rules, standard instructions, distances, running times, and other important information must be available for instant recall. There are many methods intended to assist in memorization. One of the best is to frequently use the information that is to be memorized. Using the information generally involves understanding and knowing how to apply it.

Much of the information a dispatcher must memorize is used frequently. Information that is used frequently is easy to remember.

> APPROACH Proceed prepared to stop at the next signal. Trains exceeding medium speed must begin reduction to Medium Speed as soon as the engine passes the Approach signal.
>
> MEDIUM SPEED: Not exceeding 30 m.p.h.

These rules are among the many that a train dispatcher must know. Several methods and memory enhancing devices can be used to assist memorization. Memorizing the words may be required, but memorizing the meaning is the intent. If the dispatcher remains aware of the effect of an Approach signal on trains, the memorization will follow.

> *If this freight train goes to Fargo to clear, he'll be in the clear at 0450. That puts the passenger train 3 minutes away – he'll see the approach signal, but it will clear up before he passes and needs to start slowing. Here we go....*

Or

> *If this freight train goes to Fargo to clear, he'll be in the clear at 0450. The passenger train is going to be passing the approach signal right about that time but the speed limit is 30 through there, so it won't hurt.*

The same principle applies to all of the information that a train dispatcher must commit to memory. Consciously make use of the information until you know it.

Train dispatchers must also commit to memory some information that is seldom used. Recognize which information must be memorized but is seldom used and create a use for it. When not reviewing the dynamic information such as train location and track maintenance work that is authorized, create situations that require application of seldom-used rules and procedures. Pick a train on the territory. Invent a situation: it derails, must inspect then set out a bad order car, has a hazardous material leak, is encountering signal problems, or anything else that comes to mind. Look up all of the rules and procedures that apply to the situation. This procedure helps with memorization of seldom-needed rules and instructions. It also helps with recognizing situations in which a seldom-used rule or instruction applies, when memory alone may not be sufficient, and where to look for the applicable information.

IF YOU DIDN'T WRITE IT DOWN, YOU DON'T KNOW IT

That sounds a bit extreme, but there is a lot of truth in that statement. The train dispatcher must know a large volume of dynamic information. Constant review is the key to knowing and remembering. You can't review what you haven't written down.

DO IT NOW!

Remembering as much as possible of the current situation is beneficial. It is essential to a proficient train dispatcher. Do not, however, trust important information to memory, especially if the information absolutely must be shared with someone else later. If a hazardous situation is reported, protect it immediately even if no trains are expected to pass. The condition may not be corrected as soon as anticipated. Perhaps the intermittent signal trouble turns out to be a broken rail. Now the **SECTION** (track maintenance, from the name for the territory assigned to a maintenance crew) forces must be called. Hours pass and the note on the desk is just another of many. A train that was four hours away when the trouble was reported is about to show up at the broken rail with nothing on it. Perhaps the section crew hasn't shown up yet at transfer time. The note about the broken rail is forgotten, left to be found somewhere on the trainsheet or in the live file. In the meantime, the relief dispatcher has a derailment after allowing a train to pass over the broken rail. Even if it appears silly, cover it now!

Put out the appropriate protection immediately upon notification of a hazardous situation. In territory that uses one of the forms of written authority, issue the restriction on the appropriate form, Track Bulletin, Track Warrant, Form D, or whatever it may be called, to every train that holds authority to pass the hazardous location.

> MAIN TRACK OUT OF SERVICE AT MP 339.7
>
> FLAGS ARE NOT DISPLAYED

If there are no trains on the road, address the restriction to trains at terminals either side of the problem. If necessary, address the restriction to the dispatcher. Addressing the restriction to the dispatcher may be necessary if trains are on the road but have not yet been authorized to pass through the restricted area. In CTC, establish blocking and protect in writing in some way. The protection may be issuing a permit to the dispatcher, addressing the Track Warrant, Track Bulletin or other form of restriction to the dispatcher, or establishing the blocking and writing a tag with the reason for the blocking.

Whatever means is appropriate for the situation, don't delay protecting a hazardous condition. Protect it now.

21. KEEPING THE LINE OPEN

Railroads can continue operation through weather that brings other modes of transportation to a complete standstill. Trains can often operate normally through dense fog, blinding rain, sleet, and heavy snow. Depending upon the type of cars in the train, trains may operate normally in winds in excess of 50 m.p.h. There are some ways in which weather can suddenly bring operation to a halt:

- In extremely hot weather, rail expansion may cause the track to move sideways, forming a sunkink.
- In extremely cold weather, rail contraction may cause the rail to break, leaving a gap (**PULL APART**).
- Snow and ice may build up in switch points making it impossible to change the position of the switch.
- Low-lying areas may flood.
- Landslides or avalanches may block the track from above.
- The subgrade may slide downhill (**SLIPOUT**).
- The subgrade may completely eroded away by moving water (**WASHOUT**).
- Very high winds can blow cars out of a moving train and off the track.

Dispatchers should be aware of the type of weather disruption to which their territory is susceptible. Often, the difference between keeping the line open and a shutdown that continues for days rests largely with the train dispatcher's awareness of developing problems.

GENERAL

During severe weather ask trains for condition reports frequently. Ask specifically about locations where experience indicates that problems may arise.

Be suspicious of the abnormal, especially if weather is severe. In CTC territory, a momentary track occupancy indication could be a sign of a pull apart (the rail is broken, but as the track continues to move it makes contact just enough to restore the signals), or a washout (the high water and debris momentarily provide a path between the rails for the signal current just before washing the ballast and subgrade away). Dispatchers should also be aware that such an indication might be a sign of vandalism or sabotage. That situation is not related to weather, but it may be related to remoteness, inaccessibility, and location not readily visible to many people.

Maintenance of way forces should be available and patrolling normally damage-susceptible areas during severe weather and during periods of flooding. If those forces are not available and reports from trains or others in the field cause even a slight concern about the safety of train operation, call the appropriate authority, present the information, and request track and structure inspection. Do not allow trains to operate through an area or over a structure when reasonable evidence indicates that a hazard exists. If a train must be operated when the condition is unusual but the hazard is not known, require movement at restricted speed. If any defect is visible to the train, do not authorize further movement. Train crews, operating officers, signal maintenance employees and others could once exercise judgment about the safety of moving a train over defective track. The Federal Track Safety Standards specify the class of employee authorized to determine the safety of train movement over defective track. No others may establish the safety of the situation and allow movement.

RAIN

In mountainous territory, consider that if a train at a high elevation reports heavy rain, that there may be flash flooding at susceptible lower-altitude locations many miles away. Continuous rain of long duration may cause or aggravate flooding, generally at expected locations, along non-mountainous lines. During severe weather, ask train crews to report conditions that could result in a problem including unusually heavy water runoff, unusually fast current in streams, and unusual accumulation of water. A culvert plugged with debris can result in flooded track or washed-out subgrade in a very short time. Report unusual conditions in the greatest detail possible to the responsible maintenance of way supervisor.

Heavy rains may also cause landslides (mudslides, rockslides). Areas in which landslides are expected are generally protected with a slide fence. A slide fence consists of fence posts and one or more horizontal wires. The wires carry the low voltage current of a signal circuit. If a landslide breaks or disconnects the wire, the circuit is interrupted causing block signals to show their most restrictive indication.

Signal and track maintenance forces may not be able to use access roads and trails normally used to avoid needing time on the track. They may also not be able to use roads to move about the territory.

SNOW

Switches are the railroad's points of greatest vulnerability to snow. A train does not have great difficulty with snow several feet deep over the track, but a few inches of snow in a switch can bring operation to a standstill. Railroads are also susceptible to snow accumulating in cuts. A railroad may pass through a hill in a very deep cut in order to maintain a reasonable grade.

Where snow accumulation in switches is normal, power switches are generally equipped with heaters or with hot or cold air blowers intended to keep points clear of snow accumulation. Except during the most severe snowstorms, the reliability of these switches need not generally be a consideration. Severe snowstorms with high winds can overwhelm these devices and cause trouble. Where switches are heated, ice can be a problem when the heaters are turned off after a storm or if the heater fails during a storm.

Dispatchers should pay close attention to winter weather. The ability to operate trains normally can deteriorate very rapidly. Failure to recognize signs of trouble can result in a complete tieup of the line. Obtain frequent condition reports from trains. Specific points of interest are heavy snowfall (an experienced train crew may even estimate accumulation rate for you in inches per hour), high wind and blowing snow, sleet or freezing rain, and drifting snow or snow accumulating in cuts. A train can successfully run through several feet of snow, but the snow needs somewhere to go when the engine pushes it away. Trains may have difficulty with deep snow accumulation in long cuts and on extended stretches of flat terrain. If forces to handle potential problem conditions are not already on duty, the supervisor should be called and given a detailed description of the conditions. If the forces are already on duty, the dispatcher should keep them informed of the latest condition reports so that they can arrange to be where they are most needed.

If weather conditions are causing a problem for trains, the support services needed to keep the line open may not be able to use the highways. There are several implications for a train dispatcher.

Signal maintainers and track forces may need to use the track to move about the territory. They will become the most important traffic on the line. Forces keeping the line open should not be held for train traffic (a different situation from maintenance cleaning and plowing occurring after a storm).

The vehicles these forces use may not be able to move readily, or at all, through the snow. It may be necessary to provide transportation on locomotives. Moving maintenance forces to where they need to be as the situation changes will require some unusual considerations when planning train movements.

Crew vans handling relief crews may not be able to reach trains. Crews may need to be transported to trains on locomotives, which might be special light engine movements. The difficulty involved in obtaining a relief crew should be considered carefully. Plan carefully and provide the longest possible notice to the crew office. Avoid using the same slim margin against the hours of service limit that might be tried under normal conditions. Plan crew relief for populated areas. At a minimum, there should be somewhere for the crew to go for shelter if the locomotive fails. If possible, the location should have some type of facility for meals.

Train and engine crews for normal or relief service may not be available at all or may be unreliable in reporting for duty. Don't make decisions based on having a crew until they are on hand at the terminal. That includes crews for hours of service relief. Don't tie up the railroad with a dead train stopped in a tactically poor position because of an assumption about crew availability. It is not good practice under normal circumstances, but it is much more important in severe winter weather.

Problems must be anticipated to the greatest extent possible.

Consideration must be given to the possibility of a train being snowed in when delayed. Long duration standoff meets should be avoided. Inform the crew of the first train to arrive well in advance of the possible extended delay. Have them adjust their arrival accordingly if possible. If traffic dictates that a train is put away for an extended period, consider that the location might be unavailable until well after the storm subsides. Under similar conditions, trains have been immobilized for days afterward.

Solicit frequent reports from train crews and maintenance forces. Important information includes reports of switch heaters or blowers that appear inoperative or are not keeping up with snow accumulation, sidings that have significant accumulation, areas of drifting, and accumulated snow obscuring signals. If a train has local work at a station, determine the conditions at that station from other traffic before the arrival of the train with local work. If switches must be dug out, arrange for maintenance of way forces to do so before the arrival of the train if possible. If not, or if snow accumulation over the tracks to be used will make the movement difficult or dangerous, instruct the crew to take the setout cars through to another station and/or leave the pickup cars. A train that spends an extended time digging out switches or plowing tracks with the engine so cars can be shoved into them may be snowed in.

Maintenance forces on duty only for snow control are sometimes called **SNOWMEN**. They may be assigned to a specific location, or to patrol the territory by train as directed by the dispatcher. The dispatcher must plan the use of the snowmen in conjunction with the train movements. If a meet will take place at a siding that has not been used for some time or that other trains report the switches are snowed in, the dispatcher should arrange for snowmen on the first train to arrive at the meet if possible. Planning should include awareness of the potential for problems at selected meeting points and the number and location of the available snowmen. Remember that these people have no facilities available to them except the locomotive cabs. If they cannot be relieved after a reasonable period, arrange for food, water, coffee and other supplies to be brought to them, arranging rendezvous between the snowmen and the supplies. Do not, under any circumstances, leave the snowmen without a train. If they are left in anticipation of a meet and problems prevent either train from arriving, they will be left in the elements with no shelter.

Operating trains frequently is an important method of keeping the line open during heavy snow. If normal traffic is not sufficient, light engines can be operated in addition to or in lieu of normal traffic. Trains, whether regular traffic or light engines ordered to keep the line clear, should be operated through sidings with sufficient frequency to keep snow accumulation from making them impassable.

COLD

Extreme cold has several significant effects:

Resistance to movement is greater, especially in a stopped train. Assume that trains will not start as easily or quickly as they would under normal conditions. Assume that each train may perform as though it is heavier than the tonnage shown (by perhaps 5 or more tons per car depending upon the temperature).

Airbrakes can have problems caused by leakage or by blockage by ice. Charging the brake system will take much longer than normal. Trains may need to be shorter than normal because of increased leakage. Don't make decisions based on the normal amount of time in the terminal if the temperature has decreased significantly, if the size of the train has been increased, or if the train is originating. It may be necessary to remove cars from the train in order to reduce brakepipe leakage to an acceptable level. The process may take much longer than anticipated. It is generally prudent under those circumstances to remove cars from the train 25 or more at a time. Terminal managers may make much smaller individual reductions in train size attempting to move the maximum possible number of cars, however. If this procedure is followed, the delay could be many hours. The hours of service limitation is an important consideration. Long terminal delay may cause an hours of service relief on the road under undesirable or hazardous conditions. Relieving crews in the initial terminal after a long delay may exhaust the crew supply, leaving an accumulation of trains in the terminal and/or trains tied up on the road without crews for hours of service relief.

Rail is under greater than normal tension and may be brittle. Broken rails may occur much more readily in extreme cold weather. The rail may contract away from the break, making repair take much longer. Reduced train speeds may be required in extreme cold weather. Repaired broken rails may have additional restrictions. The report from a train of an unusual rough spot in the track should be investigated. The rough ride may have been caused by a broken rail that has perhaps not been detected by the signal system, by a rail breaking as the locomotive passed over, or by a track condition that could lead to a broken rail under normal traffic in extreme cold weather.

Employees will be less able to work outside for extended periods of time. Dispatchers should consider the conditions when planning train movements and maintenance work. Among the effects of extreme cold, ordinary maintenance work may take longer than usual because of the inability to work outside continuously for extended periods.

HEAT

The sunkink is the effect of heat that most affects train operation. The rails on main tracks are often continuously welded and have no expansion joints. The temperature is considered carefully when welded rail is put into place so that the effect of expansion and contraction will be minimized. The track structure - ballast, ties, and fasteners - is designed to contain the force of the expanding rails and prevent the track from moving laterally. If the conditions were not entirely correct when the rail was laid, or if there is weakness in the track structure such as an insufficient amount of ballast or an insufficient number of fastenings, the track may be forced out of alignment laterally, sometimes by several feet. An emergency brake application by a heavy train moving at a moderate speed combined with the effects of heat may also cause forces that exceed the strength of the track structure and cause the track to move out of alignment. Any time the ballast is disturbed, such as after surface correction or the installation of new ties, that section of the track is subject to sunkinks. Track maintenance forces may set a slow order speed for one or several trains after such work. The weight and movement of the trains stabilizes the track, allowing subsequent trains to move at higher (but less than normal) speed. The movement of an approaching train may also increase the force on the track sufficiently to cause lateral movement. Train speeds may be restricted in extreme hot weather to reduce the possibility of this effect.

The report from a train of an unusual rough spot in the track should be investigated. The rough ride may be caused by track that is moving laterally or by a condition that will allow lateral movement. Once such a condition develops, a severe sunkink can occur rapidly, even under a passing train. A train stopped by an emergency brake application in extreme hot weather should be reported to track maintenance forces.

Ordinary maintenance work may take longer than normal. Employees may not be able to work for the same extended periods that they might under normal conditions, and additional care must be used to ensure that the work being performed does not weaken the track structure and cause a sunkink.

22. FAILURES AND PROBLEMS

The first sign of trouble is generally the report that the train has gone into emergency. This is known as an undesired emergency application. A defective airbrake component, a failed airbrake component, an uncoupled air hose, a broken knuckle, a broken drawbar or draft gear, or a derailment could cause it. If there are adjacent tracks, assume that a derailment has the adjacent tracks blocked and stop trains on the adjacent tracks. Also assume that the derailment has damaged tracks behind the train and handle the next train appropriately. See the procedures in the next chapter: EMERGENCY! Continue to protect the adjacent tracks and the track behind until you have been notified that there has been no derailment. If the conductor finds a cause and has not reached the end of the train, there may be other problems. Some conductors may continue to look if experience tells them that there may be additional problems and perhaps derailed equipment. Some railroads may require inspection of the entire train before it is moved. Under some conditions, an emergency brake application on a heavy freight train can damage track. If there are instructions to inspect the track after any emergency application, start the inspector immediately.

The best-laid plans of the dispatcher are worthless at this point. First, the crew must ascertain why the train stopped. The engineer will first try to **RECOVER THE AIR**, by putting the brake control in the release position and waiting for the air pressure to build. Sometimes defective brake components cause an emergency brake application for no apparent reason and the brakes will release as soon as air pressure has been restored. If the air does not recover within a few minutes, a crewmember must walk along the train looking for a failed component. Once the failure has been found, it must be corrected.

The dispatcher must begin improvising train movements until the amount of time required is better known. If the trainline is not separated, the engineer should see pressure building within a few minutes. It may be possible to release the brakes after about five minutes, but the brake system may not be fully charged for twenty minutes or more. The engineer will decide whether the train should be moved after release is possible but before the system is fully charged and should be able to give an estimate of the time required. Advance trains from planned meeting points, if possible, using this information. Pay attention to the train that has trouble. Note the time the emergency application was reported and exactly where the engine stopped. Listen to the crew on the radio. Note the time that the conductor discovered the failure and where it is in the train. This information can be important to figuring when the train may move and to establishing a new plan. If the conductor calls out car numbers over the radio, write them down. They will be needed when reporting the cause of delay. Pay close attention to trains that may have trouble making the next terminal on hours of service because of the delay. If the delay will cause trains to arrive late on call figures at crew change points, notify the terminal of the delay immediately. It may be possible to delay calling the connecting crew. If the crew has not been physically called yet (the crew dispatcher has not called them on the phone), advise the terminal that you will give them a new call figure once trains are moving again.

RELATIVELY SPEAKING, IT WON'T BE LONG

The crewmember walking the train will be walking on difficult terrain along the track while looking under and between cars for a failed component. A "brisk" walk is 4 m.p.h. A crewmember looking for a failure may be walking 2 m.p.h. or less. That's about three feet per second. If the failure is 4000 feet deep in the train, it could take over 20 minutes to find it. If it is necessary to inspect the entire train, the time required to inspect before correcting the defect is better estimated: a minimum of the time it takes to walk the length of the train. It isn't possible to anticipate the delay at this point. The failure might be the car behind the engine or it might be 6000 feet back in a 6100 foot train. If the failure is a knuckle on the right end of a car, the engineer will drop a knuckle onto the ground from the locomotive, then pull the train ahead. The conductor will give the engineer a stop signal when the rear of the train is adjacent to the replacement knuckle. The forward movement will be at about 5 m.p.h., or about seven feet per second. Pulling up to the replacement knuckle will take about half the time it took to find the failure. Replacing the knuckle is generally a procedure of about 10 minutes, however it can take much longer if the knuckle pin is bent. Once the knuckle is replaced, the front of the train will be shoved back to couple with the rear portion. The return trip will also generally be at about 5 m.p.h.

If the failure is a knuckle on the wrong end of a car, it isn't possible to pull up to a replacement part for repair. Instead, the last good car is pulled up to the knuckle that has been dropped on the ground. The knuckle is loaded on whatever surface of the car will hold it, and the head end of the train is backed to where the rear is stopped. The procedure is otherwise similar to the procedure for a broken knuckle on the right end of the car.

If the failure is an uncoupled air hose, which can happen if the hose is too short or hangs too low, the train will generally be ready to go once the failure is found. In some cases it may be necessary to place a dummy hose (a short piece of air hose with a coupling on each end) between the hoses attached to each car. If there is no dummy hose on the engine (spare hoses are carried but often not dummy hoses) the failure may recur. In some cases the failure may have been caused by a broken bracket holding the hose to the car, requiring a temporary repair by tying with a piece of wire. The next crew change point should be notified of temporary repair or the need for material in advance so that the necessary material can be available when the train arrives. Often, if uncoupled air hoses require this type of repair, the conductor will recouple the hose then ask permission to back the train to have the engine at the con-ductor's location to obtain the necessary tools or parts. Sometimes an air hose bursts and must be replaced. If the conductor anticipated the need for an air hose and a pipe wrench, the failure will not take long to correct. If the conductor needs a hose and a wrench from the engine, the time needed will be similar to that needed to replace a broken knuckle on the wrong end of a car.

Once the train is coupled, the crew may ask for permission to back up to pick up the conductor. The rulebooks of various railroads may make different provisions for this movement. It will probably be important for the dis-patcher to know exactly where the train is situated and its relationship to public or private grade crossings, signals, and other features. The reverse movement may be made faster than when backing up to the rear of the train, perhaps at 10 to 15 m.p.h., or about 15 to 23 feet per second. The walk of 20 minutes is reduced to a backup movement of three minutes. If the reverse movement cannot be authorized, the conductor will spend about as long walking up as it took to find the break. It may be possible to move the train forward, with the conductor riding one of the cars, to a point at which a reverse movement can be authorized.

IT WILL BE A LONG TIME

Sometimes a failure may cause a break at more than one place in the train. Since both crewmembers are on the front of the train, a second failure may not be apparent until the first has been repaired. This will be a surprise. The new problems caused by the second failure cannot be anticipated or avoided.

If the conductor finds that the failure is not a knuckle, but rather a drawbar, the delay will undoubtedly be a long one. The crew cannot repair a failed drawbar (and may not have sufficient personnel to remove it from the track). If the drawbar is out on the right end, the train must pull ahead to the next track on which the car can be set out. The conductor will probably be riding the last car, so the movement may be only 20 m.p.h. or so. If there is room for all of the cars on the track, the crew will probably leave all of them and return with only the engine. This will be much faster than shoving the train with the conductor riding the lead car. Once the engine has returned to the rear of the train, the damaged drawbar may need to be removed from between the rails, provided one or two people can move the part in the track. It is possible that the drawbar extends high enough above the rails to be struck by low parts of locomotives or cars and cause a derailment. If two people cannot move the drawbar, they must wait for help to arrive in the form of an officer, a car repair truck, a maintenance of way worker, or another train crew.

If the head end of the train has been left with the defective car, the rear end will be pulled up to that point and will be left on the main track. The time consumed during the return of the engine to the second part of the train will depend upon the signal system. The engine may be able to return a large part of the way at track speed, or the entire return trip may be made at restricted speed. The train dispatcher must be familiar with the characteristics of the signal system in the area in order to accurately predict the time required. Depending upon the distance, the trip with the second part of the train may be made at a higher speed than the trip with the head end because the conductor is in the engine cab instead of riding on the side of the last car. Before reassembling the train, it may be necessary to leave the defective car on another track because the track the rear end of the train is on is needed for train movement. The crew will leave the defective car, reassemble the rest of the train, then move the defective car. The car may need to be moved to another station if there is no suitable track at that location. The movement to and from that location will generally be made at close to normal speed.

If the drawbar is out on the wrong end, the magnitude of the problem and the time needed is much greater. Once the failure is found, the head end of the train must be taken to a place where it can be left clear of the main track. The engine must return to the rear of the train. The time consumed will be similar to that described above for a drawbar out of the right end of a car. Now time will move much more slowly. First, the iron (remains of the drawbar) probably must be removed from the track. After that is done (If the crew cannot do that without help, they must wait for help to arrive), the defective car must be coupled to the engine with a heavy chain or tow cable and must be uncoupled from the rest of the train. The entire process may take over 30 minutes. The defective car must then be taken to a place where it can be left clear of the main track and the engine must return to the train. The defective car will probably not have operative brakes and there will be a large amount of slack because of the tow cable or chain. The crew will probably tie a handbrake lightly to avoid excessive slack action. The movement with the defective car will probably be made relatively slowly, perhaps 20 m.p.h. The engine will probably return to the rear of the train at near normal speed, depending upon the distance and signal system. The rear end must then be pulled up to where the head end was left and the train must be doubled back together. The dispatcher should begin planning traffic as soon as the magnitude of the problem is known. Determine the distance to the next place the head end of the train can be left and the next place the defective car can be left. Figure the approximate time:

The conductor tells the engineer they got a drawbar out of the right end 40 behind the engine.

- The train is 5 miles from the next siding. 20 m.p.h. = 60 minutes for 20 miles = 6 minutes for 2 miles = 3 minutes for 1 mile. That's 15 minutes to the next siding. The car cannot be left there. The nearest track on which the car can be left is another 2 miles.
- Assume that the train was able to pull into the track, add 5 minutes for the engine to uncouple, pull out of the siding, and be ready to return to the train.
- The speed of the return trip will depend upon the distance, the signal system, and the weather conditions. The crew must be careful of colliding with the rear end of their train. For 5 miles, the return trip may average about 30 m.p.h. That is 2 minutes per mile, or about 10 minutes.
- Listen carefully for the conductor to report the progress of removing the iron from the track. 30 minutes is a reasonable amount of time to allow (if there are sufficient personnel on the crew to move it at all), but there is no way to be certain. If the crew needs help, consider the driving time of whomever is sent to help or the possible arrival time of the crew of another train. In estimating the time, consider whether the people arriving to help can drive right to the problem or must walk some distance.
- The trip back to where the head end was left will take about the same amount of time as it took for the engine to return to the train.
- Allow 5 minutes for uncoupling, coupling and releasing the brakes on the head end of the train.
- The movement of the head end of the train out of the siding and back against the rear end of the train will average about 10 m.p.h. Remember to allow an extra 400 feet each direction for pulling out past the switch. 40 cars averaging 60 feet is about 2400 feet plus pulling over the switch is about 2800 feet. 10 m.p.h. is about 15 feet per second (feet per seconds is approximately 1.5 times miles per hour; this is a very useful equivalency to remember). 2800 feet x 2 directions = 5600 feet. 5600 feet / 15 feet per second = 373

seconds. 373 seconds / 60 seconds per minute = 6 minutes. A reasonable rule-of-thumb estimate without any figuring would be 10 minutes to pick up cars and couple them to a train.

- The engine must be uncoupled from the train, pulled over the switch and coupled to the defective car for the movement to where it will be left. A rule-of-thumb estimate is 5 minutes.
- Since the drawbar is out of the right end of the car, the car will probably have brakes and will not be a safety hazard. The movement to the set out track should average about 30 m.p.h. for a 2 mile trip, or 4 minutes. If the car had the drawbar out of the wrong end and was chained to the engine, the trip would take twice as long.
- Leaving the car in the setout track will take about 5 minutes .
- The return trip will be at about the same speed as the trip from the train to the setout track (depending upon the signal system), making the return about 4 minutes. The engine has no cars in front, so the engineer will be able to see the track and the rear end of the train as it is approached.
- Coupling to the train and releasing the brakes will take about 5 minutes. If the train is on a grade, the conductor may have tied on some hand brakes to ensure that the train did not roll away if the air brakes released. That could take an additional 5 minutes per car with handbrakes tied on.

The delay to the train with the problem after finding the problem: add up the steps and the estimate is 1 hour 48 minutes. The example shows a method that can be applied to most problems trains encounter. That figure is not guaranteed, but will provide a reasonable estimate to be used in planning, moving other trains, and setting calls on connecting or relief crews.

Always stay as far ahead of the activity as possible. Don't ignore the situation for the two hours then discover when the train is ready that the crew doesn't have enough time left to make the terminal, the connecting crew has been on duty for an hour and has no train to run, and the train will cause hours of delay to other trains while waiting for a relief crew.

BE INVENTIVE

While one train is stopped because of trouble, the situation on the rest of the district may deteriorate. When possible, find ways to expedite the process of getting the train moving. Two important elements in getting things back to normal are manpower and transportation. During regular workdays, there may be maintenance of way workers in the vicinity, perhaps waiting for the train that has trouble to pass so they can go to work. Supervisors may be in the vicinity but too distant to hear the train crew on the radio. If the dispatcher knows of specific employees nearby that can help, they can be called directly. If the dispatcher knows of no one nearby, repeating what is being reported as an acknowledgment will alert nearby employees that assistance may be necessary:

> *Roger 976, in emergency just coming up to the Firville crossing, let me know what you find.*

> *Roger 976, knuckle 65 behind the engine.*

If the information is in a conversation between the crewmembers, the dispatcher can simultaneously tell the crew that the information has been heard and alert employees that may be nearby:

> *Dispatcher to 976 I got that, knuckle 65 behind the engine.*

The help of a nearby train may be enlisted if it is in a useful position behind the train in trouble or on an adjacent track of a multiple track line. If the disabled train is blocking important road crossings, sometimes a call to the local police, preempting their calls to complain, can result in a ride for a conductor headed back to the engine for a knuckle, an air hose, or tools. Describe the situation and the time that will be needed, purely as a matter of information about the blocked crossing. Let the police determine if they want to help, don't ask them to do so. If they have an interest in clearing the crossing quickly and it is apparent to them that they might be of some help, someone will show up.

23. RUNAWAY

Will you ever handle one? Probably not. Should you know what to do? Absolutely.

WHAT'S GOING TO RUN AWAY?

Runaway equipment can take one of several forms
- improperly secured cars that begin moving because of gravity, the wind, or both,
- cars that a switch crew has kicked too hard,
- cars that an industry fails to control while moving with a truck or car mover,
- cars unsecured by vandals that begin moving because of gravity, the wind, or both,
- improperly secured unattended locomotives that move on their own,
- stolen locomotives,
- improperly secured unattended trains that begin moving on their own,
- trains that the crew cannot control.

In addition to the locomotives, cars, and trains listed above, the runaway may be maintenance of way equipment such as push cars or self-propelled machines.

HOW WILL THE DISPATCHER FIND OUT ABOUT RUNAWAY EQUIPMENT?

There is a chance that someone will report:

> *You have 2 runaway cars, ABC 12345 and DEF 67890 a couple of empty 50 foot box on the main track passing through Townville headed east just a minute or two ago.*

*They were moving about 25 m.p.h. There is a really strong
southwest wind here right now.*

The chance, however, is slim.

There is a chance that the dispatcher will need to figure it out from one or
two clues. That chance is very great. Some of the clues may be
- a complaint from the public about a train where there should be
  none. The complaint could be about crossing signals not
  operating soon enough, a train with no headlight, a train moving
  too fast, or a train not whistling for a crossing,
- more than one case of signal trouble such as a CTC switch out of
  correspondence and a track occupancy in another location, a
  track occupancy in two adjacent sections, or a track occupancy
  that appears behind a train after it has cleared a section,
- background conversation on the radio that involves discussion of
  an unexpected and/or unusual train movement,
- repeated unintelligible radio calls,
- indication that a train is making exceptionally good running
  time,
- a question from a yardmaster or service facility foreman about
  the location of a certain train or locomotive that should be in the
  yard or service facility.

The train dispatcher must combine route knowledge with the clues. If a track
occupancy is left behind a train moving downhill, it will probably not be
runaway equipment. (It may be derailed cars in the train, though.) If a track
occupancy appears between two stations and there is no track connecting
with the main track or it is downhill from the main track to any connecting
tracks, it is probably not runaway equipment. That deduction is dependent
on the dispatcher being attentive and being in a position to notice whether
the track occupancy first appeared somewhere where runaway equipment is
possible.

Runaway cars or unpowered maintenance of way equipment will probably
be moving downhill, but could be moving on flat track if kicked too hard in a
yard or being propelled by a strong wind. Cars have been propelled by the

wind for over 20 miles. The dispatcher must be aware that the direction of the runaway equipment may change if the grade changes significantly.

Powered equipment moving on its own may have almost no range limit. Unlike cars moving on their own, powered equipment will probably not be stopped by an ascending grade, although the speed may decrease. Powered equipment moving on its own is possible anywhere that powered equipment has been left. That could be maintenance of way equipment or work train locomotives left in an industrial track for the night or weekend, locomotives left in an industry track to be picked up by another train, yard or road locomotives awaiting assignment, or an industry's locomotive.

Runaway trains will generally occur on moderate to heavy downhill grades.

Sometimes the first clue will raise suspicion. Sometimes the first clue will make the reality of runaway equipment obvious. Sometimes a single clue will not raise suspicion but the combination of more than one clue will. If something doesn't make sense, isn't right, seems strange, or whatever else indicates that runaway equipment is even remotely possible
- protect against possible runaway equipment,
- obtain information from any source possible.

WHAT CAN BE DONE ABOUT IT?

Handling runaway equipment is like handling a really hot train. The difference is that with a really hot train you can take a chance on a close meet and perhaps a delay. A really hot train *should* not be delayed. Runaway equipment *cannot* be delayed.

What to do will depend upon the situation. Some incidents of runaway equipment may be a non-event; over before anything serious happens. Some incidents of runaway equipment may turn into a very serious situation very quickly. Railroad workers and the public may be in extreme danger before anything can be done to warn them or to rectify the situation. The train dispatcher must quickly evaluate a situation and take the steps that will be most effective.

First, do not leave the communication equipment. If there is a headset and no speaker, do not take off the headset. Important information may be overheard rather than directed to the train dispatcher by someone who will wait patiently if there is no immediate answer. Information that is directed to the dispatcher may be time sensitive; important only at the moment the first attempt to report it is made.

GET SOME HELP

The first few minutes will be very busy. The first two steps (this section and the next) should, depending on the severity of the situation, be done simultaneously. The train dispatcher handling the territory is the obvious person to clear the line of trains and railroad employees. If possible, call a chief dispatcher or other supervisor or a dispatcher from another territory to assist with notifying the public. A maintenance of way employee along the line can be helpful. They are usually very familiar with the area and may have access to a cellular phone, radio phone or even a police or fire station in a nearby town. If the train dispatcher has not obtained help in the office before reaching M of W employees while clearing the line, ask the M of W employees to help with the public notifications.

CLEAR THE LINE FOR THE RUNAWAY EQUIPMENT.

The nature and extent of this activity will be dependent, to a degree, on the nature of the runaway equipment. Powered equipment moving on its own may run for a long distance at a high rate of speed. Cars moving by wind or gravity power may stop or reverse direction because in a change in direction or grade. A runaway train may stop on an ascending or slight descending grade. Do not take a chance moving trains just one more station. All trains that have even a remote chance of being overtaken or met between stations should be put in the clear as soon as possible. If it is not possible to get a train in the clear, pick the best possible location for a collision within the confines of the time available, instruct the crew to stop at that location and get clear as quickly and as far as possible.

The runaway equipment may increase speed to a completely unexpected level. Stop all track maintenance activity that has even a remote possibility of being encountered by the runaway equipment. Line up switches as necessary and to the extent possible to avoid a derailment at an undesired location. Employees working near but not on the track may be in danger. If there has been no specific need to describe the situation on the radio, such as to notify trains or maintenance of way workers to get in the clear, broadcast the available information to inform as many employees as possible of the situation. The message should include what is known or suspected

> *There appears to be some type of equipment moving on its own southward on Main 1. It passed Townville at 0537.*

The information, whether to specific trains and M of W workers or as a general broadcast, will serve the purpose of clearing the line and may result in the assistance of employees along the line in either identifying the equipment and situation or controlling the equipment.

PROTECT THE PUBLIC

Runaway equipment may be running faster than the highest speed that crossing signals can detect and still provide adequate warning time. It will probably not be displaying a headlight that will call attention to the movement as it approaches and will probably not sound a warning for crossings or for people along the track. Runaway equipment may exceed curve speed and derail or derail at a turnout, creating a dangerous condition in the area near the track. Runaway equipment may speed past a passenger platform where people are expecting a passenger train to stop.

Derailment of runaway equipment in a curve is unpredictable. The speed at which a curve can be negotiated without derailment is dependent upon specific characteristics of the equipment involved and of the track. The best assumption for the purpose of protecting the public is that if the estimated speed of the runaway equipment is approaching 1.5 times the speed limit of a curve, it may derail. Roads adjacent to the track along the outside of a curve and housing or commercial areas adjacent to the track along the outside of a curve may be in danger until the situation is controlled. Don't assume, however, that the equipment will derail and the event will be ended at the first curve where the speed is 1.5 times the speed limit. Depending upon the nature of the equipment and the track, the runaway may exceed 3 times the curve speed limit without derailing.

The fastest response (not necessarily the most desirable response) is necessary. The railroad employs its own police force, but these people will probably not be in sufficient number nor in a suitable position. Any unfavorable publicity the railroad may receive as a result of immediate response to protect the public would be greatly exceeded if the railroad did not take steps to protect the public and damage or injury resulted. Local police should be notified immediately. The notification should include known information and a description of the hazard:

> *We have five loaded cars moving on their own along the ANB Railroad track between Townville and City. They were seen leaving Townville at 0933. We don't know how fast they are moving, but it is downhill from Townville to City and they may be moving at a high rate of speed. The cars may be moving at a much greater speed than can be detected by crossing signals. There will be no headlight. It is possible that they may overturn on the curve at the south end of City. We need your assistance. Crossings should be guarded if possible, people kept away from the track, and that stretch of highway south of City along the curve should be closed until the situation has ended.*

If passengers may be on the platform of an attended station, call the station attendant and have the passengers moved to a safe location. If the station is not attended, ask the police to move the passengers to a safe location.

If the available information indicates that someone is aboard the equipment, state that in the notification so that rescue forces will be aware should the equipment derail. If unauthorized people may be on the equipment, also state that in the notification so that the police may act appropriately when the equipment is stopped.

Warn the police that they should not attempt to board the moving equipment. Boarding moving equipment is not simple without some training. Many railroads have prohibited boarding moving equipment because even experienced and trained people have been injured. The equipment may be moving too fast to board without being apparent to the untrained eye. Boarding may be a useless endeavor. A person boarding must board at the end with a handbrake. There is no way to move to the opposite end of the car. If the runaway equipment consists of several cars, a single handbrake may not be effective and there is generally no way to move from one car to another. If the runaway equipment includes a locomotive, it may be possible for a person familiar with locomotive operation to stop the movement, but often not with any certainty. If the movement is downhill and the brakes are not connected, the locomotive brakes may be ineffective and the person who boarded to stop the movement may be in danger.

Ask the police to assist with notification of other public protection agencies that can be of assistance. Note which agencies were called and which were asked to notify others. Once the incident has ended, the alarm should be withdrawn in the same manner it was originally passed to ensure that all affected have been notified.

Once first response has been notified, or simultaneously with first response if there is enough help, notify the railroad's police.

DETERMINE THE SITUATION TO THE EXTENT POSSIBLE

Obtain the best possible information about the situation. Time the movement at any possible point and keep track of the speed. Ask employees and/or public protection agencies along the line to observe and provide information such as type of equipment, number of cars or locomotives, approximate speed, location and time, are there signs of people on the equipment, are there signs of brake application such as smoke from the wheels or glowing wheels. Obtain this information from people in position to observe as frequently as possible. The information will help project the location and behavior of the equipment and will help in the development of a solution.

STOP THE RUNAWAY EQUIPMENT

A runaway equipment incident will end in one of two ways:
• The equipment will be stopped without derailment or collision.
• There will be a derailment or collision.

The train dispatcher will probably not be able to stop the equipment without derailment or collision. The dispatcher can be instrumental in stopping the equipment, however. Stopping the equipment will be dependent on the exact situation and the skill and judgement of the employees involved. They will need the best possible information the train dispatcher can provide: equipment, speed, location, expected changes because of grades, possible points of derailment and whether people are known to be aboard the equipment.

Chasing runaway equipment with a locomotive involves a significant risk as the locomotive approaches the rear of the runaway equipment. A derailment may result if the following crew attempts to couple in a curve. As the locomotive approaches at a slightly greater speed than the runaway equipment, any sudden change of speed by the runaway equipment could result in a serious rear end collision. The change of speed could be the result of derailment or, if the airbrakes are charged and not applied, a broken airhose or undesired emergency application of some other cause. If the following locomotive couples successfully, it may not be able to stop the runaway equipment. The result would be more runaway equipment and a crew in danger. If the runaway equipment is powered by only wind or gravity, the direction may change. This is very important if the locomotive chasing from behind is at some distance when the direction changes; a serious collision could result.

Operating a locomotive in advance of runaway equipment with the intent of coupling and forcing the equipment to a stop is perhaps more dangerous than attempting to stop the equipment from the rear. Matching speed from ahead of the equipment will be difficult. A failure to couple on the first attempt may result in a derailment more easily than a failure to couple at the rear. A failure to match speed can result in a serious or even catastrophic collision between the runaway equipment and the locomotive attempting to stop it.

All personnel involved should carefully consider the situation before taking action. The train dispatcher should ensure to the degree possible that those in the field have considered all possibilities when developing a plan to stop the equipment. By being too close to the problem, they may have over-looked curves, grades, populated areas and other important considerations.

Derailing runaway equipment can be as benign as running a slow-moving empty car over a derail or into a stub-end track. It can be as serious as a spectacular derailment involving the loss of life and/or property. Derailing the equipment may not be easy. At high speeds, heavy equipment may break block derails. Power switches are either Normal or Reverse. They cannot be left "cocked" or "split" with the intention of causing a derailment. Running the equipment through a switch in the reverse position may result in derailment, but it may not. Running equipment into a stub-end track may not be effective at high speed. Runaway equipment has remained upright for a great distance beyond the end of the track before crashing through a building and stopping.

Derailing runaway equipment is very serious business. There can be great undesired consequences. Cars could travel rather a great distance from the track. Cars may contain hazardous material that could be released as a result of the derailment. The derailment may result in a fire. These are all of primary importance when planning a derailment.

From the outset, the train dispatcher should begin identifying good and bad places for a derailment. A planned derailment should be as far as possible from

- highway crossings,
- parallel highways,
- rivers, streams, and bodies of water,
- residential or commercial development along the track,
- hazardous material storage or manufacture facilities,
- overhead or undergrade bridges,
- parks or other non-developed areas where people may be gathered,

- places where contractors and other non-employees may be working near the track such as in or adjacent to an intermodal yard. Information about and control over the whereabouts of contractors and others may not be as effective as it is for railroad employees.

If the best possible location is not available, use the best possible of the choices available. Allow enough time, if possible, to allow evacuation of the area if necessary. If possible, do not allow runaway equipment to pass a good derailment location in hopes of stopping it later if allowing the runaway equipment to continue may significantly increase the danger of the situation. This is especially important where only a few locations may be suitable for a derailment.

Consider the possibility of people on board the equipment. Stopping the runaway equipment without collision or derailment may require greater consideration if there are people on the equipment. The people on the equipment may be the crew that has lost control of the train, incapacitated railroad employees, industrial employees on or in the cars when they got away, or the vandals that released the equipment.

The train dispatcher may be in a position to set up the collision or derailment that will stop the runaway equipment, but probably not. If it appears that collision with a preceding or opposing train is inevitable, stop that train in the best possible location considering the available time and instruct the crew to evacuate. All decisions should involve the train dispatcher and personnel handling the situation in the field so that no one is caught in a dangerous situation by surprise. Public safety agencies should be informed of the decision to stop the runaway by collision or derailment when possible to ensure that the area will be secure from bystanders, residents, motorists and others that may be affected. The situation should be ended in the most deliberate and well-thought manner possible.

24. EMERGENCY!

There is a common element among infantry soldiers, police officers, fire fighters, train and engine crews, and train dispatchers. You can work for hour after boring routine hour and suddenly experience your worst nightmare. A train will hit an automobile which burst into flames with the occupants still inside, a train will derail accompanied by fire and hazardous material release, a passenger train will derail or a mad gunman will be shooting passengers and employees. People you know may be involved, you may hear that they or others have been killed or seriously injured. Whatever has happened, you don't do anybody any good if you cannot handle it. You don't do the people at the other end of the conversation any good if you are adding to the chaos that they are experiencing. You must do the opposite. Inside, your heart may be jumping into your throat. Outside, you will do the most good for all concerned if you sound like this is just another boring thing to deal with.

DERAILMENTS AND COLLISIONS

FIRST AND MOST IMPORTANT

The first and most important element is

PROTECT THE WRECK.

This cannot be overemphasized. Acknowledge the radio transmission or telephone call reporting the incident, then if there is any chance of secondary collision with another train, get it stopped. If your railroad is adjacent to another railroad or another dispatcher's territory, get your colleague at that dispatching office on the phone immediately. If there is an overhead or undergrade bridge with another railroad or another dispatcher's district that has a possibility of being involved, do the same. The same applies to adjacent highways. If you know or suspect that a highway is blocked with derailed railroad equipment, call the local police or highway patrol immediately. Tell them what you know and tell them to hold the line while you get more, but get protection moving toward the derailment immediately. Without a caboose and employees on it to watch the track behind the train, a derailed car may be dragged for many miles, damaging switches and road crossings and partially turning rails along the way. Unless the derailment was obviously caused by a local incident such as striking a vehicle on a crossing, stop the first train behind. Until there is definitive evidence that the track behind the derailment is not damaged, the first train should be instructed to proceed at restricted speed and to watch for evidence of derailment.

If the emergency involves a derailment and you are handling CTC, if you can do so by changing signal indications while performing the emergency related duties, stop approaching trains beyond the second siding from the derailment or beyond the second controlled crossovers from the derailment on multiple track.

GET SOME HELP

If you are working in an office that has a chief dispatcher, assistant chief dispatcher, corridor manager or some equivalent, call for that supervisor because you will probably need help, depending upon the magnitude of the problem. If the incident is a collision with an automobile or pedestrian, the only thing left to do (directly related to the incident) after notifying the chief dispatcher or equivalent is to wait for the authorities to release the train. If the incident is a derailment, the work has just begun. If you have a terminal for the information system at your position, run a list of the train and send it to a printer. The information in the list may be essential to understanding the seriousness of the situation. The list on the monitor will not be useful as you or the supervisor will need to make notes about car position, fire, hazardous material or other information. The supervisor, a clerk, or one of your colleagues in the office can get the list from the printer and bring it to your desk. Do not leave the communication equipment. If there is only a headset and no speaker on the communication equipment, do not take off the headset.

If you are on another district in the same office, your work location is nearby, you see or hear that there is an emergency, and you are able to leave your position, offer to run lists or help with the immediately needed notifications. Time can be critical in the first few minutes of an incident.

SEND SOME HELP

Return to the radio or telephone and get all of the information that is available. The most important elements of the additional information will be injury, persons trapped, fire, hazardous material release, involvement with highways and buildings along the line where non-railroad personnel may be trapped. Get this information first. If you do not already know the exact location, find out now. If you are not familiar with the location, try to get a good description from the person on the radio or telephone and see if the person reporting can tell you how to direct emergency services to the location. While getting the information, if the emergency services dispatcher is not already on the line from step one, make the call. If they answer while you are still receiving information, keep them on the line with "ABC Railroad dispatcher with a serious [car/train collision, train collision, derailment] with [injuries, fire, hazardous material emission, etc.] near Yourville stand by I'm getting more." If a passenger train is derailed, make sure to state that a passenger train is involved. Give the emergency services dispatcher the information including a description of how to get there. Include the apparent nature and extent of injuries and how many people may require aid. If a passenger train is involved, give the emergency services dispatcher the best possible description of the derailed equipment; upright, turned over, down the bank, accordion, in the water, buried, etc. If there is fire, tell the emergency services dispatcher what is or may be on fire. Here is where the list comes in handy. If the fire is reported near the back/front/middle of the train, look on the list for hazardous material that may be involved and tell the emergency services dispatcher of the possibility. If occupied passenger cars are on fire, be sure to state that fact. The additional minutes needed for help to arrive because the equipment could not find the incident, there was not enough equipment, or it was not the right equipment can be very important to someone involved in the incident. The time you have saved the emergency services with this information may save someone's life.

GET SOME INFORMATION

The emergency is handled, now it is time to handle the incident. Get the exact situation. The chief dispatcher or other supervisor should be there by now to help with the questions, but generally they will look something like this

- Is the power all on the rail?
- Is the lead unit damaged (especially important if the train has struck a vehicle at a crossing)?
- How many cars on the ground?
- Where in your train?
- How do they lay (upright, leaning, turned over, crosswise, buried, etc.)?
- Did you notice anything before the air went?
- How fast were you moving?

The answers to these questions will help determine what equipment and supplies are necessary. The most accurate possible answers at this point may save many hours of delay waiting for rerailing forces and supervisors to arrive just to find out that they have inadequate equipment for the task. The list you printed in the first few seconds will be useful now. The response you get on the radio once a crewmember has started to walk back may be something like

> *The last car I can find is RBOX 199099.*

And maybe subsequently

> *Now I have a MILW 7865 on the rail and so far looks ok from there.*

When each train had an occupied caboose, information about the nature and extent of the derailment was somewhat easier to obtain. The employees in the caboose could see evidence of a derailment behind the train. They might have prevented a much more serious derailment by stopping the train at the first sign of damage to the track. Once the train stopped, a crewmember on the caboose would start walking toward the head end to assess the situation. If the track is passable, the engines from a following train can be cut off and run light to the rear of the derailed train. The movement should be made at restricted speed with the caution that the track may be damaged and may be blocked by derailed equipment not in line with the track and not displaying a marker. On arrival, the crew of the light engine can assess the condition of the train from the rear. Eventually, they will be needed to pull the portion of the rear of the train that is not derailed back to the next siding or yard track, or on a multiple track railroad to a place between crossovers.

The rest of the incident response and the required notifications will be the chief dispatcher's responsibility. You will be very busy with the next steps for a while. You will, however, probably be the only source of communication to the scene for some time. Handling information to and from the scene is important and requires prompt attention.

NOTIFY TERMINALS AND DISPATCHERS ON ADJOINING DISTRICTS

Contact the dispatchers either side of your district and the terminals either side or within your district with a figure on the first train that will be affected by the incident:

> *1175 got a car at Crossingville, looks like 0830 up to you and everything else behind.*

For affected trains in the opposite direction, something like:

> *"1175 got a car at Crossingville, 262 is first behind it not up to you until 1115.*

If it looks like the line will be shut down for an extended period of time, then the information will be something like:

> *1175 is in the ditch at Crossingville, I'm not going to let anything out of Terminaltown yet until we see what we've got.*

They can now start their own planning process using the same information you have.

START PLANNING

Start shutting down the district in an organized manner based on the magnitude of the incident. A crossing collision or pedestrian struck by a train will not require shutting down the railroad, but it will change the entire plan of operation. If the incident is not fatal and there is no damage to the lead unit, the delay will be roughly an hour. If the incident results in a fatality, the delay may be over two hours. If the lead unit is damaged, the delay might include cutting the power away from the train, proceeding to a place where the order of the units can be changed and returning or it might include awaiting the arrival of another unit. If the incident is a derailment, a reasonable initial estimate is an hour per derailed car after rerailing begins. If the track is destroyed, cars sideways and plowed in, twice that is a good place to start.

Passenger Trains

If passenger trains will be affected by the incident, consider the passengers when staging the traffic. Passengers may need to be transferred to alternative transportation. Food or other supplies may be necessary if the delay will be long. Emergency services may need to reach the train. Under normal operating conditions, the movement of the passenger train can be used to reduce the response time. The passenger train can move toward the emergency responders. The chance of needing emergency services for a staged passenger train is not great, but it should be considered. The emergency responders must always go to the train if it is stationary. When possible, stop passenger trains at a passenger station. If not, stop them at a location close to a crossing with a main road. The train can be spotted on the road to unload passengers. Notify the agency responsible for customer service, describe the options, and determine the course of action. Notify passenger train crews of the plans for handling their trains and passengers. Do not let passenger train crews tie up on hours of service while passengers are on the train. Ensure that a relief crew is ordered sufficiently in advance. If no relief crew is available, send a transportation supervisor, such as a trainmaster, or send a freight service crew as a last resort.

The Interruption Will Be Short

CHECK REMAINING CREW SERVICE HOURS AND RELIEF CREW AVAILABILITY.

If the interruption will be short and operation will continue normally within a few hours, the first thing to consider is hours of service. You do not want to add to the congestion with dead trains. Start a worst-case plan; maybe the auto collision will turn out to involve a fatal injury and the train will be hung for four hours. Figure a plan for all of the traffic if the line opens in four hours. Check all of the crews for time left to work. Count the number that can't make it if the delay is four hours, even if they receive no delay after the line opens. Count the number of trains that will make it with two hours left. Depending upon the normal local procedure, contact the crew office or have the chief dispatcher contact the crew office and find out if they are in a position to provide crews to relieve trains from the first count and from the second count. If the answer is yes, it is time to begin figuring a crew relief plan. Find out how many vehicles are available and how many crews can be transported in each vehicle. (If the crew office answer is no to either, it is time to start figuring an organized partial shutdown plan.) The planning process can be complex. It can also be iterative, requiring several tries to achieve a plan that will work.

CREW RELIEF PLAN

Order a crew for each of the trains that can't make it. You don't know yet where it will take place, but you know it will. The crews will require some amount of time to report, even if the call is for Soon As Possible. Some crewmembers may take the entire notification period to which they are entitled, so start the calling process immediately.

Match the report and driving times and the time the crew to be relieved has to work against places the relief crew can drive to. Select places at which the dead train will be in the clear or on a multiple track line places between crossovers where other traffic can pass. Consider the location of road crossings. The crew on the train may not have time to cut crossings, generally a time-consuming procedure. Unless it is absolutely unavoidable, do not plan to stop the train on the main track for relief. If there is any doubt that the crew can make it into the clear somewhere before running out of time, consider exchanging crews with a train that can be left clear of the main track.

If the crew relief can be done in the clear, continue with the rest of the plan, working the relieved trains into the other traffic after a worst-case scenario time for the crew to arrive and assume responsibility for the train. If the crew relief can absolutely not be done in the clear the choices are:

- Set a location that has the least effect on other traffic.
- If the crew is coming from the opposite direction, go as far toward the relief crew as possible. If the crew is coming from behind, avoid moving the train away from the overtaking crew.
- Once the plan is established for the crews called for trains that cannot possibly make it, the second level of planning establishes what to do with the crews that may not make it. Track resources have been established for the first group of trains. The trains that may not make it are planned around those allocations. The goal of the plan will be
  - protect the schedule of important trains and guaranteed service,
  - minimize the number of crews that must be relieved,
  - minimize the delay waiting for relief crews.

Do not tie up terminals with trains that do not have time to finish whatever work is necessary on arrival without a plan that has been created jointly with terminal personnel.

If the normal terminal procedure is a main line crew change, the terminal may be able to absorb several trains following closely that have only a short time left to work. Care must be exercised in these cases. Part of the quick processing of the main line change trains is leaving promptly. If the dispatcher on the adjoining territory cannot take the fleet of arriving trains promptly, the last ones in line may not have time to pull up to the crew change location before running out of time. This could result in a crew on duty for a train that cannot arrive and other trains behind it that cannot pass.

A penalty payment to the outbound crew may be necessary if they are required to relieve the arriving train short of the terminal. A crew that leaves the terminal to relieve a train at a location on another crew district then passes through the terminal onto its assigned district may be entitled to an additional day's pay or some other payment. Other crews may also be entitled to a payment of some amount if they were available and not used. It is also possible that the outbound crew cannot relieve the arriving train short of the terminal at all, perhaps because of not being qualified on the territory.

Trains that must work in the terminal should have time remaining to perform the normal arrival procedure such as pull into a receiving track, set the air on the train for inspection, cut the power away from the train and perhaps take the power to the service facility. If the arriving crew does not have time to perform these tasks, the yard will need to devote a yard crew normally assigned to other work to finishing the work of the arriving train crew. This could affect schedule performance of trains, and also affect the ability to accommodate the following trains.

Once a plan has been formulated, present it to the terminal and to the adjoining dispatcher if trains will be changing crews and leaving immediately. Find out if your plan works for them or if it needs more refinement. The information is given informally and may be followed with some discussion and some adjustments.

> *Looks like when this breaks up they'll come to you like this:*
>
> *482 at 0915 with two hours to work,*
>
> *612 at 0925 with 30 minutes to work,*
>
> *5002 0930 with 35 minutes to work,*
>
> *4486 1015 with an hour to work.*

Several possible responses may include:

> *OK, this will work.*
>
> *Can you get 482 behind 5002?*

Can you get 482 behind 612?

I can't deal with 612 [and/or 5002] with only that much time.

Can you take 1137 out first, he'll be ready about 0900.

I'm sitting on two of them that aren't called yet and one on duty at 0900. I can't take anybody before 1030.

You now have the basis for the necessary revisions to the plan. The other required information is the answer to the earlier question about crews available to relieve trains that will have two hours or less to work on arrival, and the number of vehicles available to transport crews. The result of this exchange may be one of the following:

- hold 482 somewhere for 612 and 5002,
- relieve 482 as a result of holding for 612 and/or 5002 (possibly necessary because of interaction with opposing traffic),
- relieve 612 and / or 5002,
- relieve 482 and 612,
- relieve 4486 because of the need to get 1137 out,
- relieve 612 then relieve 5002 4 hours later because transportation is only available for one crew.

The point is, the possible number of solutions is very large. It is possible that you will need to present another version of the plan for consideration before a workable solution is developed. The plan you eventually execute must work for the adjoining dispatcher districts and terminals and must work for the crew dispatchers or you might as well not have a plan.

Call the crews necessary to support the plan. Don't delay the call. Don't try to save a relief crew by making a change that affects adjoining dispatcher districts or terminals without checking the new plan with the people involved. The congestion following a service interruption creates a delicate situation. A small change in situation without a complete workable plan for handling it can result in a complete shutdown. Trains may be stopped on the main track with no crew available and no way of moving other traffic.

Once the plan has been developed and the crews have been called, it must be executed with precision. Every part of the plan must be monitored. It is important under normal conditions. It is critical when there has been a service interruption. The slightest deviation can result in a complete change and perhaps in a significant problem that could result in another shutdown of operation. If a crew has not reported at the expected time, or transportation is not available as expected, or a relief crew does not show up at the relief location as expected, or a train does not pass a station as expected:

- Find out why.
- Determine if the situation requires correction or can be corrected.
- Figure a revised plan based upon the previous step.
- Notify everyone concerned of the unavoidable change.
- Do not allow a surprise failure to turn the plan for operation into an unintended shutdown if at all possible.

PARTIAL SHUTDOWN PLAN

A partial shutdown plan consists of tying up one or more trains awaiting the ability to run them. Avoid allowing trains to tie up at an unplanned location if at all possible. On a single track line, leave a siding open between tied-down trains whenever possible. On a multiple track line, leave a two track section open between tied-down trains whenever possible.

Each tied-down train should be at a location accessible by highway. Where weather or terrain prevents access by highway anywhere, relief crews must arrive by rail. The train transporting the crew may be a regularly operating train or it may be a light engine operated for the express purpose of relieving one or more crews. The time required for rail transport and the movement of the train bearing the relief crew must be included in the operating plan.

BEFORE THE LINE REOPENS

If the closure will be temporary and crews will remain on duty, whenever possible stop trains where restaurants, convenience stores or similar services are available. If some trains cannot be left at such a place but will pass one before arriving at the waiting point, offer the crew the opportunity to stop long enough to make a purchase should they desire.

The Interruption will be Long

A reasonable estimate of the amount of time the line will be closed is an hour per derailed car from the time the wrecking forces arrive. If there is fire or a hazmat problem, additional time will be needed; probably an hour per car after the fire or hazmat situation has been addressed. If the cars are sideways or buried, two hours per car is a reasonable figure.

If the line is to be shut down, that is all traffic stopped awaiting the ability to move traffic, the shutdown should be as orderly as possible. Reopening the line must be considered when shutting the line down.

If possible, leave one siding or one section between crossovers on a multiple track line open either side of the incident that closed the line. If the incident was a derailment, these sidings will probably be needed for the cars in the train that were not derailed and for rerailing and/or track repair equipment and for rerailed cars.

If possible, tie down trains no closer together than every other siding or every other section between crossovers on a multiple track line. The open sidings or sections of multiple track will be needed to meet trains once the line reopens.

All passing should be accomplished while shutting down the railroad. If possible, tie down trains in the order of importance; most important closest to the point of closure. A recovery plan that involves holding some trains to be passed by others will extend the length of the service disruption. It could result in further congestion and possibly another closure if the crew supply becomes exhausted attempting to execute a poorly conceived plan.

Consider the disposition of crews carefully before transporting them. Determine whether crews should be returned to the home terminal, continue to the away terminal, or tied up at a suitable on-line location (allowed by the hours of service law if there is an unpredictable occurrence such as a derailment).

Whenever possible, tie trains down where there is road access to both ends of the train. A highway vehicle may be helpful if the train has been standing long enough to require a new rear end device battery or if a brake test is required. If a train must be left where there is no road access to either end of the train and it is necessary to remove the crew by use of the locomotive, make a record of the track and location at which the locomotive was left. If it was necessary to cut crossings when tying the train down, make a record.

If the temperature is below freezing, moving locomotives to a place at which they can be fueled and watched for continued operation may be necessary. Leaving units unattended for an extended time in below freezing temperature should be avoided. If the locomotive is damaged by freezing after an unexpected shutdown or automatically drains after an unexpected shutdown, it will be a surprise when a crew is sent to the train and the recovery plan will probably require complete restructuring.

Before the crew leaves a locomotive, whether left on the train or at some other location, ask for the fuel level for each unit and make a record. Idling locomotives burn three to six gallons of fuel per hour. If the consumption for the locomotives involved is not available, use six gallons per hour. Estimate the time remaining before the idling units will run out of fuel and make a record.

If possible, determine the time on the rear end device battery and record it. Consider the need for fresh batteries once traffic is released. It may be necessary to instruct crews to take the battery with them for charging. If the battery or rear end device is removed from the train, make a record.

Cancel any movement authority the crew possesses and instruct the crew to remove all movement documents such as Track Warrants, Forms D, Track Bulletins or whatever other form the railroad uses to authorize train movements or issue train movement instructions. Instruct the crew to leave the train documents such as the list, wheel report, and hazardous material handling papers in a secure place in the locomotive and make a record of where the documents were left. Ask the crew about handbrakes, blocking, skates or other means of securing the train and make a record.

Make a record of the disposition of the crew, whether sent on to the distant terminal, returned to the on duty point, or tied up in a hotel along the line.

If the derailment has occurred during a snowstorm and trains may be drifted in while tied down, consider running around the trains and sending them back to a terminal. Once they have drifted in, clearing the line may be extremely difficult. Drifted in trains will aggravate the derailment and snow conditions for a much longer time.

In addition to making records on the (paper or electronic) trainsheet, begin a single list of all of the trains and their condition. List each tied down train by direction in order from the closest to the most distant from the derailment. Show all of the important information described above. Copies of this list should be furnished to the chief dispatcher or other supervisor that will be involved in establishing a recovery plan.

Starting Up After a Long Service Interruption

The supervisors working at the derailment will publish line-open figures. There will probably be several. As time moves on and the line remains blocked, the figures may become increasingly optimistic. Everyone involved is under great pressure to bring operation back to normal. Unfortunately, the pressure has the opposite effect. All too often, the recovery from a derailment looks like this (an aggregate of experiences, not the description of a single incident):

> Supervisors at the wreck state at 0600 that the track will be open at 1000. Crews are called for all of the trains tied down on the line, to be in position ready to go at 1000. Some time after 1000 the wrecking forces will be finished **PUNCHING A HOLE THROUGH THE WRECK** (getting the line open sufficiently to begin moving trains). Trains will not be able to move because the track forces couldn't finish the track while the wrecking forces were working. In an effort to clear things up as quickly as possible, someone will decide that as soon as the line is open, several trains will move as a fleet in one direction, then all of the trains in the opposite direction will move.
>
> The track will be good for ten mph. or less past the wreck. The first train will pass the wreck site and the wrecking and track forces will need the track to continue working. There is still much to do after a

hole is punched through the wreck. Some of the work will be necessary to support the movement of additional trains or movement at a higher speed. Some of the work will be necessary because until all work is concluded and all forces and equipment are released, derailments are very expensive; often more than $10,000 per hour. Generally, either the work will continue for some period of time between trains of the fleet moving in one direction, spreading them, or several trains will be allowed to pass in one direction, then the line will be closed for an hour or more for work to continue before trains in the opposite direction can move.

Many crews that have been on duty since 0800 in anticipation of moving fleets of trains will run short of time and eventually tie up on hours of service; some without moving the train. The large number of crews on the road at one time and the large number of hours of service tieups will result in the board being depleted. Crews will need to get in, tied up, and rested before the expired crews can be relieved.

Terminals will not be able to accommodate the approaching fleet of trains because of saturation with trains being held in the yard. Trains will not be able to leave because the crew supply is on the road. Crews will not be able to get in and tied up without leaving their trains on line because the terminal is saturated. These trains will aggravate the congestion caused by the wreck.

The vehicles available for transporting crews will be completely engaged, with some crews waiting on trains because transportation is not available.

Some of the crews will report to a location where there is a train and no locomotive. Some crews will arrive at the train and be expected to leave promptly but will find out that there are crossings cut, brakes tied on, the rear end device battery is dead, or that one or more units are out of fuel. Some trains will leave the place they were tied down and run out of fuel on the line somewhere, blocking other traffic.

Recovery may go on for days. Traffic may stop completely one or more times because the supply of crews has been completely exhausted.

A detailed recovery plan should be in place a minimum of 6 hours before the line is open. The plan should consider:

- The chance that the track might not open at the time specified is great,
- The first train may be restricted to walking speed past the wreck,
- The rest of the trains for the first day may be restricted to 10 m.p.h. past the wreck,
- Work will continue for many hours after the track is opened the first time. Wrecking and track forces may need one or more hours between trains for the first day after the opening of the line,
- Track or signal damage may cause all trains to operate at restricted speed between control points or sidings either side of the wreck for an extended period,
- Terminals may be saturated with trains being held because of the wreck. It may be necessary to call some trains out before approaching trains can be accommodated,
- The number of vehicles available to transport crews may limit the ability to move trains.

Start with an accurate assessment of crews on hand at each terminal, crews on hand on the road if any are tied up on line, vehicles available to transport crews, and drivers. A protracted recovery will require more drivers than vehicles.

The plan should be in place before the "final" line open figure is issued. Use the time 0000 as the line open time rather than any of the published figures. Figure all events from this time. Events taking place before opening will have negative numbers, such as -0300. It will be easy to translate this plan into current time when the "final" line open figure is announced. If the line is to be open at 1030, a -0300 event occurs at 0730; a 0500 event occurs at 1530.

Figure the train movements first. Figure the first train through using a conservative figure and considering all of the possible speed restrictions. Establish a meeting point and time with each opposing train. Figure the first opposing train based on when the initial train will let it out. It may seem counterproductive when a large amount of traffic is standing, but for the first opposing train moved select one that will arrive at the derailment site an hour after the first train passes. There is a great chance that the second train through will be held for more work if it arrives too soon. Continue planning meeting points and times for every train on the line. To the extent possible, arrange arrivals at terminals

- an hour or more apart for trains working at the terminal,
- at least twice the running time between crossovers or sidings on the adjoining district for trains that only change crew and leave.

Make the most accurate possible assessment of the time required between crew call and moving for each train. This will be affected by the time required to obtain movement authority, the driving distance and time, the accessibility of the train to a highway vehicle, the location of the locomotives and the train, how many handbrakes are tied on, whether the rear end device or battery must be replaced, and if there are crossings to cut. Figure times conservatively.

Develop a plan for crews and vehicles. Make sure there are sufficient crews and vehicles to operate as planned. Spreading trains as described should contribute to having sufficient resources.

Give the terminal and the dispatching district either side of the wreck a lineup using 0000 + time figures. Determine if the trains can be accommodated as planned. Find out what trains must be taken out and when. Work these trains into the crew and train movement plan. Establish a definite meeting point and time for each meet until all trains tied up on line have been moved.

Re-figure the crew plan including the trains that will be moved from terminals. Some of these crews may need to be called before crews called to move trains tied up on line.

Publish the plan in advance, in 0000 base time, to the supervisor in charge at the wreck site. Ensure that the recovery plan is realistic for the anticipated situation at the time of opening. Determine if **WORK TRAINS** (trains operated to perform railroad maintenance or wrecking work) or **HOSPITAL TRAINS** (wrecked equipment that has been repaired only enough to allow movement to a shop) will be needed and approximately when in 0000 base time. Add these movements to the completed plan. Again, figure a definite meeting point and time for all of these movements with each train it will encounter. Figure the time expected to be required at the wreck site and the movement between the wreck site and the track where the train will clear.

Publish the plan, in 0000 base time, complete with trains to be moved from terminals during the recovery, to terminals, crew dispatchers, and adjoining dispatcher districts. Make sure that the people in charge of crew transportation are given the plan.

This work should all be complete before the "final" line opening figure is given by supervisors at the wreck site.

From the time of the derailment until the line is opened for traffic, the track is out of service for all movements except those directed by the officer in charge of the wrecking operation. This arrangement is often not formalized by train movement documents, but it is accepted nonetheless. Once trains not related to rerailing and track repair begin to move, that arrangement is no longer acceptable. Before the line is opened and crews are called, determine a foreman in charge at the wreck site and issue authority for work under traffic. Ensure that sufficient time is allowed to place flags as necessary and have the authority hanging before the first crews come on duty. The work may continue with the least possible disruption to train traffic if the trains are allowed to proceed up to the wreck site and obtain permission to pass.

Anticipate the need for slow track instructions. Determine in advance from a supervisor at the wreck site what speed restrictions will be in effect. If it is not possible to obtain a number from the field before it is time to begin fixing trains, put out a 5 mph restriction flags not placed (flags not placed or displayed, when added to the wording of a temporary speed restriction, tells the crew that the speed restriction is in effect even without the required flags or signs along the track). It is much easier and safer to take down a restriction or increase the speed of a restriction than it is to try to put out a restriction after a number of crews are on duty and on the way to the trains.

Consider changes very carefully before making them. When resources are stretched to the limit and the line is full to saturation, a change in plan can have numerous and generally undesirable secondary effects.

Train dispatchers generally do not have the authority to enforce the procedures outlined above. If the situation is shaping up to be similar to the initial example, the dispatcher cannot do more than suggest an alternative. If that fails, do not let the confusion of the situation cause you to create or fall into a hazardous situation. The first concern should be safe operation. The second concern is efficient operation. If relieved of the second, then consider only the first.

MEDICAL AND POLICE EMERGENCIES

Railroads pass through uninhabited and inaccessible areas where emergency services are not readily available. In populated and accessible areas, the distance to emergency services varies. The movement of the train can be used to reduce emergency response time. The train dispatcher knows travel time along the railroad. The emergency services dispatcher knows the location of responders and approximate response times for the area. Combine the expertise. Do not decide where the emergency response should be sent. The location you choose, even if it seems entirely logical, may not be the closest available help.

Obtain the most complete possible information about the situation. If it is a medical emergency, get a general description of the person, the symptoms, and any first aid action being performed. If it is a police emergency, get a description of the situation such as drunk, disorderly, or armed person or persons involved.

ON A MOVING TRAIN

If the emergency is on a moving train, obtain the train's exact location. The procedure for reporting to the emergency services is similar to that described in the "Send Some Help" section, but specify that the emergency is on a moving train. Give the trains's current location and direction. Do not use timetable direction. If the track is relatively straight and the compass direction at that location is known, use it. Most of the time, the best description is

moving toward thistown from thattown.

Work with the emergency services dispatcher to determine the fastest response location. If the train is moving away from the closest help, the train should be stopped at the closest accessible place. If the train is moving toward the closest help, determine if a meet between the train and responders moving in the opposite direction will be more appropriate than having the responders wait for the train. A minute or two may be the difference between life and death.

NOT ON A MOVING TRAIN

An emergency not on a moving train may include medical or police emergencies involving track maintenance personnel, emergency situations along the track encountered by trains or track maintenance personnel, or a medical emergency involving the engineer of a train. If the location is inaccessible by road, emergency responders may need rail transportation to reach the scene. Determine the amount and nature of equipment that the emergency responders must bring to the site. Arrange for a locomotive or hirail vehicle to meet the emergency services at a specific location. Do not authorize emergency responders to drive highway or off-road vehicles on the track. If such movement is necessary, send an appropriate maintenance of way supervisor to authorize and supervise the movement.

25. RUN THE RAILROAD, DON'T LET IT RUN YOU

Railroads do not run themselves very well. If they did, there would be no need for train dispatchers. Records can be automated. Signals can be automated. Switches can be thrown remotely from the locomotive. Meets can be arranged by a computer or by train crews. Many of the things that are part of the train dispatcher's job can be performed adequately in some other way. The combination of all of them cannot.

The difference between economical and reliable railroad operation and adequately performed functions is a proficient train dispatcher who is running the railroad. Merely responding to events and adequately performing series of tasks will not lead to economical and reliable operation and is not train dispatching.

The three most important elements of train dispatching are

Anticipate,

Anticipate,

Anticipate.

Everything the district needs to operate efficiently should be ready and available when it is needed, or before it is needed when possible. Catching up is more work than being ready.

Traffic should always be operated according to a plan. When the situation changes, it is much easier and more efficient to modify an existing plan than to continue to improvise without concern for the general outcome. Handling traffic without a plan will generate one crisis situation after another. Planning and handling traffic in an organized manner is much less work and much more productive than continual crisis management.

Ensure that everyone associated with the trains on the district always has the needed information. Expect the same from them. Surprises are not a Good Thing. Don't cause them and don't quietly accept them.

Never shortcut rules or procedures and don't encourage or allow those in your domain to do so.

When emergency situations arise, maintain a composed manner that will help those in the field remain calm and address the situation at hand.

Be thorough in every activity related to train movement.

Know your limit and don't cross it.

An effective train dispatcher is authoritative, not autocratic. An effective train dispatcher must be respected. Listen to the voices of experience and the voices of people out in the field with perhaps a better assessment of the situation than can be had in the office. Consider alternatives carefully. Issue instructions. If necessary, acknowledge that the instruction is not consistent with the advice. If the decision was wrong, take responsibility - and learn from it. This will be the path to respect. Threats, sarcasm and shouting, or indecision will not.

GLOSSARY